Tudors, Stuarts and Georgians

Geoffrey Middleton

Illustrated with contemporary pictures and by Peter Dennis and T.A.S. Limited

Longman

Introduction

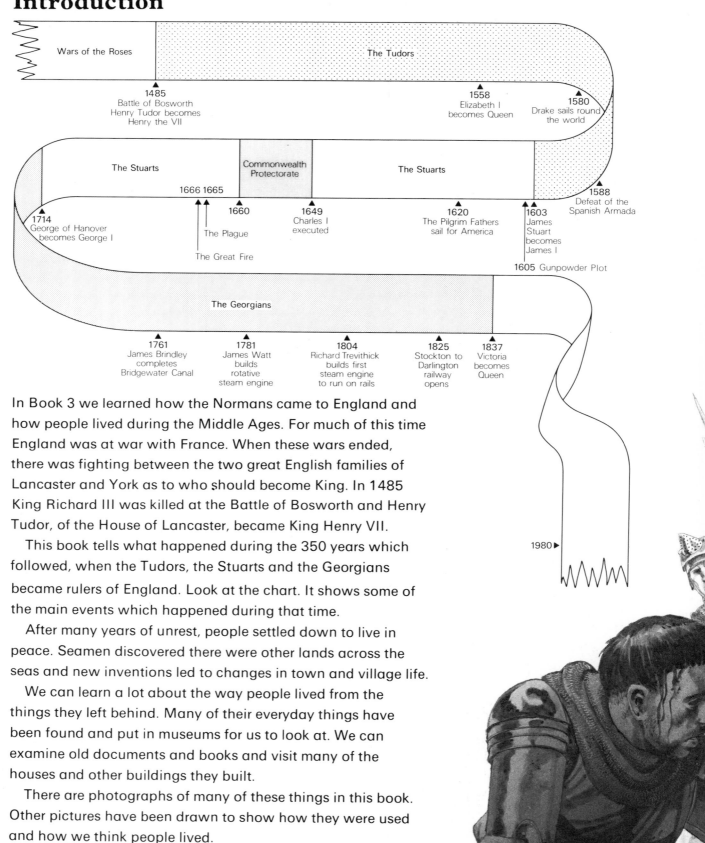

Wars of the Roses

The Tudors

1485
Battle of Bosworth
Henry Tudor becomes
Henry the VII

1558
Elizabeth I
becomes Queen

1580
Drake sails round
the world

The Stuarts

Commonwealth
Protectorate

The Stuarts

1666 1665

1588
Defeat of the
Spanish Armada

1714
George of Hanover
becomes George I

The Plague

1660

The Great Fire

1649
Charles I
executed

1620
The Pilgrim Fathers
sail for America

1603
James
Stuart
becomes
James I

1605 Gunpowder Plot

The Georgians

1761
James Brindley
completes
Bridgewater Canal

1781
James Watt
builds
rotative
steam engine

1804
Richard Trevithick
builds first
steam engine
to run on rails

1825
Stockton to
Darlington
railway
opens

1837
Victoria
becomes
Queen

1980 ▶

In Book 3 we learned how the Normans came to England and
how people lived during the Middle Ages. For much of this time
England was at war with France. When these wars ended,
there was fighting between the two great English families of
Lancaster and York as to who should become King. In 1485
King Richard III was killed at the Battle of Bosworth and Henry
Tudor, of the House of Lancaster, became King Henry VII.

This book tells what happened during the 350 years which
followed, when the Tudors, the Stuarts and the Georgians
became rulers of England. Look at the chart. It shows some of
the main events which happened during that time.

After many years of unrest, people settled down to live in
peace. Seamen discovered there were other lands across the
seas and new inventions led to changes in town and village life.

We can learn a lot about the way people lived from the
things they left behind. Many of their everyday things have
been found and put in museums for us to look at. We can
examine old documents and books and visit many of the
houses and other buildings they built.

There are photographs of many of these things in this book.
Other pictures have been drawn to show how they were used
and how we think people lived.

The war against France had lasted on and off for over 100 years. Sometimes France was winning and sometimes England. There were also times when the two countries were at peace, but only until the war broke out again.

The picture below shows the Battle of Agincourt. This was one of the battles won by the English through the skill of their longbowmen. But by 1453 the French had driven the English out of France, except at Calais, and the Hundred Years' War had come to an end.

Almost at once more fighting broke out in England between the two great families of York and Lancaster. Each had its own badge – a white rose for York and a red rose for Lancaster. Barons and knights, returning from the war in France, joined in the fighting. This War of the Roses, as it was called, lasted for 30 years and many nobles were killed. But the armies were not very large and fighting did not go on all the time. There were parts of England, too, which saw no fighting at all.

In 1485 it came to an end. At the Battle of Bosworth King Richard III was killed and Henry Tudor, fighting for the Lancastrians, was crowned King Henry VII.

Richard III

Tudor Kings and Queens of England

Henry VII (1485 to 1509) was the first of the Tudor Kings and Queens who ruled England for the next 118 years. The people were glad to have a king who could keep peace after the many years of fighting. Henry made the remaining nobles keep the law and heavily fined any who attempted to keep private armies.

Henry married Elizabeth of York and so joined together the two families of York and Lancaster, who had fought so bitterly against each other. He brought traders, merchants and lawyers into his government and encouraged trade and shipbuilding. When Henry VII died in 1509, England had become a prosperous and peaceful country.

When Henry VII died, his 17 year old son, Henry, became **King Henry VIII (1509 to 1547)**. He was handsome, clever, rich, strong-willed and often cruel.

In the past, everyone in England had been a Catholic, with the Pope in Rome as Head of the Catholic Church. Even kings were supposed to obey him. Now some people who were Protestants wanted to change some of the Catholic customs.

Henry himself quarrelled with the Pope because he would not allow him to divorce his first wife, Katherine of Aragon, and marry Anne Boleyn. So Henry disobeyed the Pope, married Anne and made himself Head of the Church in England. He closed monasteries as he feared the monks would stay loyal to the Pope. Henry took over their lands and put their gold and silver plate into his treasury.

Henry VIII was married six times, but when he died in 1547 only three of his children were still alive. They were Edward, Mary and Elizabeth.

Edward was only 9 years old when he became **King Edward VI (1547 to 1553)**, so a Council governed the country for him until he was old enough to rule by himself.

Edward was a Protestant and during his reign the Latin prayer book was rewritten in English and stained glass windows and wall paintings were removed from the churches.

Edward had never had good health and in 1553, when he was 16, he became ill and died.

After Edward's death, his elder sister became **Queen Mary I (1553 to 1558)**. Mary was a Catholic and did all she could to make England a Catholic country again and to restore the Pope as Head of the Church. She brought back the Latin prayer book and services and released Catholic bishops who had been imprisoned in the Tower of London during Edward's reign.

There were many Protestants who would not accept the Pope's authority and Mary had them put to death. During her reign of only 5 years about 300 people, including Archbishop Cranmer and Bishops Ridley and Latimer, were burned to death at the stake.

In 1558 **Elizabeth Tudor (1558 to 1603)** became Queen. She was a Protestant and in 1554, when there was a plot against her sister Mary, Elizabeth had been taken down the Thames by barge through Traitors' Gate to the Tower. It was only Mary's mercy that had saved her sister from being executed. Later she was released.

Elizabeth ruled England wisely and firmly for 45 years. The Protestants and Catholics could now live together peacefully, but during her reign there were several plots against her life. The Catholics tried to put her cousin, Mary, Queen of Scots, on the throne so Elizabeth kept her a prisoner for nearly 20 years. In 1588 Elizabeth had to agree to her execution when another plot was discovered.

During Elizabeth's reign there were many great men. There were daring seamen like John Hawkins, Sir Walter Raleigh and Sir Francis Drake, who was the first Englishman to sail round the world. There were fine writers, too, such as William Shakespeare, Francis Bacon and Edmund Spenser.

Elizabeth was the last of the Tudor Kings and Queens. She was loved by her people and she cared for them, whether they were rich or poor.

Tudor villages

During the Middle Ages most of the villagers had worked for their lords as payment for their strips of land. But after the Black Death there was a shortage of labour, for in some villages most of the people had died. Landowners were unable to get labourers to work for them. So they were glad to let some of their land as farms, for rent.

By Tudor times, the villagers worked for wages for whom they chose and paid their rent in money, as shown in this picture. Some with only a few acres of land earned the money for their rent by working for one of the better off farmers, called yeomen.

By then, more food was needed to feed the growing population. Yeomen, who worked hard and sold their wheat and barley at the local market for a good profit, became very rich. Some built themselves new farmhouses.

This yeoman's farmhouse was originally in Midhurst in Sussex. It was carefully taken down and rebuilt in the Open Air Museum at Singleton, near Chichester.

Downstairs is a kitchen and a 'parlour'. Upstairs there are two bedrooms reached by a steep ladder. There is a smoke outlet from the chimney in the centre of the house, which leads to a smoke room which was used for curing bacon.

The peasants still lived in simple cottages like these. In winter time the animals were brought inside, too.

Notice:
—the roofs thatched with straw
—the walls of mud and the windows with no glass. The peasants sat with their families outside the cottages, even in bad weather, for it was dark inside.
—the fruit trees and plots of vegetables
—the scraggy chickens.

The peasants rarely got enough food to eat and were often hungry.

Flemish weavers had come to England during the Middle Ages and taught the English how to make cloth. By early Tudor times, English cloth was in great demand all over Europe, so many farmers found it more profitable to rear sheep than to grow crops. They fenced in, or enclosed, their land and also parts of the common land to make new sheep runs.

The farmers sold the fleece from their sheep to a merchant. He washed and sorted the thick wool and brought it back to the village to be spun into yarn and woven into cloth.

Look at these two women at work. One is using a spiked board, called a carder, to brush out the thick, tangled wool into separate fibres. The other woman is spinning, or twisting, the woollen fibres into yarn.

Weaving was harder work and was nearly always done by the men. They wove the long, woollen yarn into cloth on a loom. The picture below of a weaver at work is taken from an old manuscript.

The peasants and their families were glad of the spinning and weaving when there was no work on the farms. Now that many farmers were rearing sheep there was little work for the labourers, for a shepherd and his dog could look after the sheep for most of the year.

Many peasants were unable to pay their rent or the high cost of food and wandered away from the village to search for work elsewhere. Some became beggars and thieves. They were put in the stocks, whipped or branded with a hot iron if they were caught stealing.

By the time of Queen Elizabeth, there were so many vagrants and rogues roaming about the country that new laws were passed, which said the poor must be sent back to the villages where they were born. Each parish had to collect money to look after them and find them work.

But some farmers still grew crops in the open fields. Others exchanged strips of land so their land could be together in one place.

Growing corn was still one of the farmer's most important jobs. Barley, rye and wheat were the main crops grown.

Look at this picture of work on a farm in September. This is the beginning of the farmer's year when he is preparing for the next year's crops.

Notice:
—the man ploughing with two horses, at the back of the picture
—the man in a red hat sowing the seed. Much of it must have been wasted.
—the man with two horses pulling the harrow. Its sharp teeth are pulling up the soil to cover the seeds.

In this picture farm workers are harvesting the corn. Look at the man cutting the corn with a sickle. It is hard work and very slow. Two workers have already sat down for a rest and their midday meal. What do you think the woman is bringing them? What else can you find in the picture?

After the harvest the corn was threshed with flails. These were two pieces of wood fastened together with a piece of leather. The corn was beaten with the flail to separate the grain from the chaff. The farmers and other villagers still had to pay for the corn to be ground into flour at the manor mill. People in villages made their own bread, but it was much darker than the bread we eat today.

The villagers hoped for a good harvest to provide them with enough food for themselves and their animals and, perhaps, a small surplus to sell at the market.

This picture shows a village in December.
Notice:

—the man chopping wood. The most important jobs during the winter months were gathering and chopping wood, for wood fires were the only way of keeping warm.

—the man, woman and baby inside the house

—the cow looking out of the open doorway at the far end of the house. In the autumn many animals were slaughtered, as there was not enough food to feed them through the long winter months.

—the windmill across the fields. What was this used for?

In every village there were many skilled craftsmen. There were joiners who made furniture, coopers who made tubs and barrels, wheelwrights who made wheels for the carts and wagons, potters who made jugs, bowls and storage jars and many other craftsmen. Each one took a pride in his skill and the part he played in the life of the village.

A village blacksmith at work. The blacksmith not only shoed the horses, but also sharpened the farmers' ploughs and made tools like forks, billhooks, sickles and scythes.

Things to do

1 Start to make your own book about the Tudors. Draw pictures and write notes about:
   a) sheep farming
   b) spinning and weaving
   c) ploughing, sowing and harrowing
   d) the village in winter
   e) craftsmen in the village.

2 Make a large wall picture of harvesting the corn.

3 Make models of:
   a) a yeoman's farmhouse
   b) a peasant's cottage.

4 Use books in your library to find out more about the Tudor Kings and Queens.

Manor houses and mansions

During Tudor times many lords and landowners became wealthy, after taking over lands which had belonged to the monasteries. Some of them either enlarged their manor houses or built new ones.

This half-timbered manor house is Gawsworth Hall in Cheshire. It was once the home of Mary Fitton who was Maid of Honour to Queen Elizabeth I.

Like many manor houses of that time, it was originally built on a square plan around a courtyard. This picture shows the entrance on the north side of the house. Look at the tall chimney stacks. Can you find the shield of arms on the right hand stack? This was the badge of the Fitton family and underneath it an inscription tells us it was carved in 1570. Gawsworth Hall, like many other manor houses, had a tall gatehouse at the entrance to the drive.

Not all the new manor houses were built of timber and stone. Earlier, bricks had been brought from Flanders, but by now they were being made in some parts of this country.

Barham Manor in Suffolk was built of brick. The manor had belonged to the monks at Ely until Henry VIII closed the monasteries. It is believed the new manor house, on the left, was built soon after 1545. Notice:

—the many octagonal Tudor chimneys. Instead of one fireplace in the hall as previously, now many rooms had fireplaces.

—the small-paned window frames which were made of specially moulded bricks, instead of stone as before

—the three attic windows, which were added to the house about 300 years later.

Barham Manor

This fine Tudor mansion is Hardwick Hall in Derbyshire. It was begun in 1591 by Elizabeth, Countess of Shrewsbury, or 'Bess of Hardwick' as she was called. It was completed six years later. Can you find Elizabeth's initials at the top of the four great towers?

Bess had first married at the age of 12 and by the time her fourth husband, the Earl of Shrewsbury, died in 1590 she had become a very rich woman.

Great country houses like Hardwick Hall were built of brick and stone by the nobles and wealthy landowners of Tudor England. Find the main entrance. By now the entrance was usually put in the middle at the front of the house. Wings to the house and windows were built each side of the entrance and made a symmetrical pattern. Look at the huge windows which become taller towards the top of the house. The small panes of glass are held together with strips of lead. Most Tudor mansions had large windows and in some rooms they stretched from floor to ceiling.

Inside the houses, the walls were covered with tapestries or wood panelling. The doorposts and staircases leading to rooms in the upper storeys were beautifully carved. The ceilings were decorated with plaster patterns and moulded pictures of birds and animals.

Most Tudor houses had a long gallery like this one at Hardwick Hall. This was used for walking, recreation and games when the weather was bad. Sometimes important guests were received here.

This is the Great Hall of an Elizabethan mansion called Parham, in Sussex. The household ate their meals here. Find the two windows above the carved oak screen at the end of the Hall. The steward, who was responsible for the running of the house, could look through these to see what was happening.

Tudor furniture

In Tudor times people began to have more furniture in their homes. But even so, their rooms looked very bare compared with ours today. Tudor furniture was solid and heavy and most of it was made by local carpenters from timber close at hand.

When Rychard Churche, a wealthy landowner in Nantwich, died in 1592, an inventory of his belongings included 'bedstocks and bedding – £13. 6s. 8d.' (£13.33) and 'tables, cupboards, stools, chairs, coffers, chests and other household stuff – £4'. Notice that the beds were the most valuable pieces of furniture in the house. They were often handed down from father to son.

Beds like this were called four-poster beds.
Notice:
—the tester, or roof
—the four bedposts which held up the tester and headboard
—the carving on the bedposts and headboard
—the hangings, or curtains, which were drawn at night to keep out draughts
—the feather mattress which rested on a network of strings across the bed frame. There were no springs.

Not all beds were four-posters. In some farmhouses and cottages the best bed was a boarded bed. This was made like a shallow wooden box on four short legs and contained a straw mattress. The better ones had a narrow shelf at the head of the bed, on which to stand a candle. Why was this dangerous?

The poor slept on the floor on a straw mattress or a rough mat, with a log under their heads for a pillow. Servants and children often slept on small beds on wheels, called truckles. These could be pushed under the big four-posters during the day.

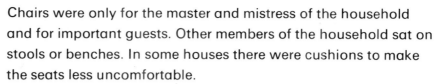

Chairs were only for the master and mistress of the household and for important guests. Other members of the household sat on stools or benches. In some houses there were cushions to make the seats less uncomfortable.

This type of chair was called a box chair. The first ones were made like a box with solid arms and a back added. The seat could be lifted and things kept inside the box, but this was often inconvenient so sometimes a door was put into the front panel. Some box chairs were very heavy and were seldom moved about, for it took several people to lift them.

This stool had a lid so that it could be used as a storage box.

Early tables were boards on trestles, which could be taken down after a meal and stood against the walls. Later, the table top was fixed to four or six heavy legs which were joined by wooden stretchers to keep the table steady. In Elizabethan times the draw leaf was invented. This could be pulled out to extend the dining table.

Cup-boards, or shelves on which drinking vessels were kept, now became enclosed to form cupboards.

This cupboard was built for Rychard Churche and his wife, Margerye, in 1577. Look at their initials and their heads which have been carved on the front of the cupboard. Look also at the carving of the royal coat of arms. Who was Queen of England at that time?

Towns

Although most people in Tudor times lived in villages and worked on the land, there were a number of towns. Although most of them were growing rapidly in size and in wealth, they were still much smaller than our towns today. London was by far the largest with a population of about 200,000. Norwich was the next largest town, though it had only about 20,000 people. Next in size to Norwich came such towns as Exeter, York, Bristol and Shrewsbury, but with only about 10,000 people living in each of them. County towns like Worcester, Durham and Leicester had no more than 2,000 people and some towns were little more than large villages. They were small enough for most people to know each other, at least by sight.

This map shows the largest towns in England at the time of Elizabeth I. Is your nearest town among them?

Below is a map of Norwich in 1559. Find:
—the castle (CC) which had been built in Norman times
—the church with its pointed spire
—the walls around the town
—the fields outside the town walls. People in towns were never far from the countryside and many went out to work in the fields. What else can you find in the picture?

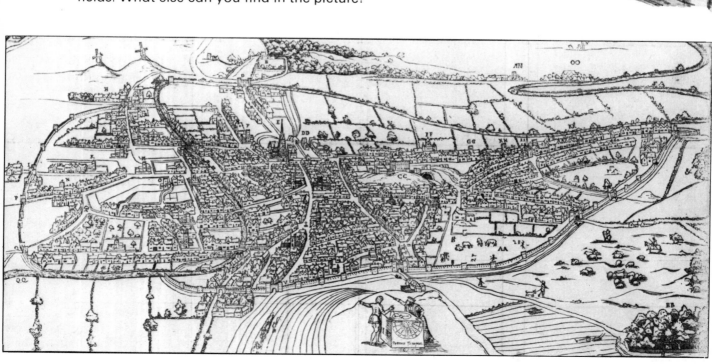

The cloth industry brought wealth to certain parts of Yorkshire, Gloucestershire and particularly East Anglia. Here, small market towns like Hadleigh, Lavenham, Sudbury and Thaxted grew into busy wool centres.

In these towns the cloth merchants built guildhalls, wool halls and fine houses. They also built or enlarged beautiful churches like this one at Lavenham in Suffolk.

Some merchants became very wealthy. When Thomas Spryng of Lavenham died in 1523, he owned 27 manors and land in 130 parishes.

Inside the towns, the streets were narrow, noisy and crowded. There were few pavements and people pushed their way among the many horses and carriages, carts and barrows. Street sellers, who could not afford a shop, walked up and down shouting their wares. Animals and poultry were driven through the busy streets to the market.

The streets were dirty and smelly, too, for people still threw their dirty water and rubbish into the gutters, as they had done in the Middle Ages. Although some drained away into nearby streams and rivers, most of it piled up in the streets, causing a risk to health. A few of the larger towns had scavengers who collected the rubbish and dumped it outside the town.

At night there was always the danger of being robbed, for the streets were unlit except where householders placed lanterns outside their houses. Some towns had bellmen, or watchmen, who patrolled the streets throughout the night.

15

In Tudor times there was no town planning. Cottages with small gardens, inns, stables and pigsties were all jumbled together with the larger houses of merchants and craftsmen.

Look at this house at Nantwich in Cheshire. It was built for Rychard Churche, a landowner at the time of Elizabeth I.

The house was built of strong oak beams which were carefully measured, cut and numbered at the craftsman's yard. Then they were fitted together with wooden pegs on the site. Spaces in the framework were filled with wattle and daub. This kept out the heat in summer and the cold and wet in winter.

In most towns the shops were clustered together in the town centre. They were at the front of the shopkeepers' houses and the workshops were at the back. People who sold the same kind of goods lived near to one another, so some streets had such names as Bread Row, Pudding Lane or Shambles, which was where the butchers lived.

Outside each shop was a sign to show what goods were for sale, or what business was carried on. Here is a picture of a tailor's shop. Can you make up a sign for it?

Food prices were fixed by the town council, who sent searchers round the shops to find out any dishonest tradesmen. Bakers who sold underweight loaves, and butchers and fishmongers who sold bad meat or fish, were fined.

Permission to hold a weekly market was granted to most towns by royal charter and usually the market was held in the open air, in the town centre. Some towns had a market hall like this one at Titchfield in Hampshire. This is now in the Open Air Museum near Chichester.

The market halls usually had an upper room which was used as a guildhall or council chamber. Below, was the open arcade where stalls were set up and goods sold. Sometimes the space behind the stairs was barred and used as a lock-up.

Animals from surrounding villages were driven along the country roads and through the crowded town streets to the market. People from miles around brought their goods to be sold.

Here a countrywoman is bringing her produce on a donkey. Two other women have already set up their stall. What are they selling?

In some of the larger towns merchants from other parts of the country and from lands across the seas came to the market.

Until Tudor times there had been no standard weights and measures, so sometimes those used by dishonest shopkeepers and tradesmen were inaccurate. Henry VIII ordered each town to have one set of accurate bronze weights and measures like these. The shopkeepers' weights could then be checked against them.

Look at these Elizabethan coins. At that time there was no paper money and all coins were made of real gold or silver. Can you see how the edges of the coins have been 'clipped'? People did this and melted down the small clippings of gold and silver for themselves. The coins became smaller and smaller and lost their shape.

In most towns there were blacksmiths, tailors, tanners, cordwainers (shoemakers), masons, carpenters, chandlers (candlemakers) and many other craftsmen. In one London street, called the Strand, there were 52 goldsmiths' shops and the houses and shops in Goldsmiths' Row were thought to be the most beautiful in England.

Look at this artist's picture of a goldsmith's workshop. Notice:

—the three goldsmiths at work. Their leather aprons catch the precious gold and silver filings.
—the two apprentices. By Elizabethan times, rules for their training were made by the Queen's Council in London. Apprentices served their masters for 7 years.
—the large windows to provide good light for their work
—the bellows near the fireplace
—the various tools on the wall.

Things to do

1 Draw pictures and write notes about:
   a) manor houses
   b) mansions
   c) town streets
   d) shops and markets
   e) craftsmen.
2 Draw a map to show the largest towns in Elizabethan times.
3 Make models of:
   a) a Tudor manor house
   b) a market hall.
4 Make a wall chart of Tudor furniture. You may find some in your local museum.
5 Paint a wall picture of a market in Tudor times.

This gold pomander, mounted with rubies and diamonds, was part of a goldsmith's hoard discovered under a house in Cheapside in London. Pomanders containing herbs and spices were carried by many people to destroy the smell of decaying rubbish in the streets. This one must have belonged to a very wealthy person.

Seamen and explorers

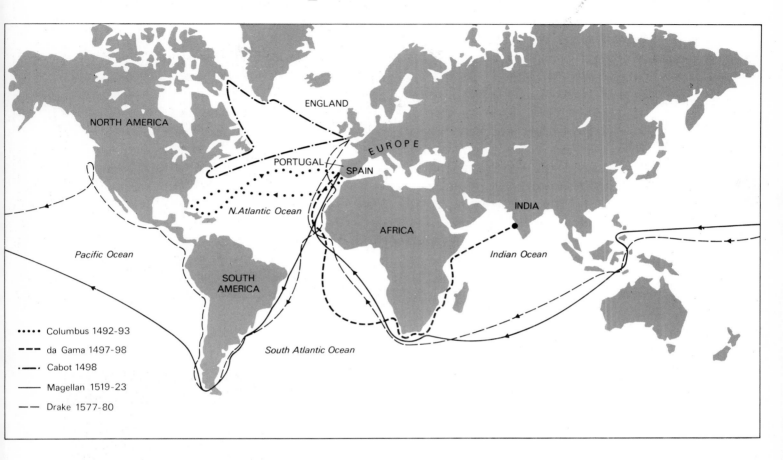

Map legend:
- •••• Columbus 1492-93
- --- da Gama 1497-98
- •—•— Cabot 1498
- —— Magellan 1519-23
- — — Drake 1577-80

Map labels: NORTH AMERICA, ENGLAND, EUROPE, PORTUGAL, SPAIN, INDIA, AFRICA, SOUTH AMERICA, N.Atlantic Ocean, Pacific Ocean, Indian Ocean, South Atlantic Ocean

During the Middle Ages merchants had brought spices, jewels and other riches from India and other Eastern countries to Europe. But the long journeys overland were difficult and dangerous. The merchants were attacked and robbed of their valuable cargoes by fierce tribesmen. So men began to look for sea routes to the East.

Look at this map which shows some of the voyages made by seamen in Tudor times. Bartholomew Diaz sailed from Portugal in 1487 and reached the southern tip of Africa, later called the Cape of Good Hope.

Five years later, an Italian seaman called Christopher Columbus persuaded the King of Spain to give him three ships to try to reach India by sailing westwards across the Atlantic.

Columbus was convinced the world was round, though at that time most people thought it flat. He failed to reach India, but found the islands we now call the West Indies. On later voyages, Columbus reached other lands on the coast of South America, which contained gold and silver mines. This made Spain the richest country in Europe.

In 1497 another Portuguese seaman, Vasco da Gama, sailed round the Cape of Good Hope and across the Indian Ocean to reach the coast of India. Soon afterwards, the Portuguese were sailing regularly backwards and forwards to India.

The same year, John Cabot also tried unsuccessfully to find the route to India by sailing westwards, but he came to Newfoundland and claimed it for England.

In 1519 Ferdinand Magellan, another Portuguese seaman, sailed across the Atlantic and down the coast of South America. Eventually, he found a passage between the rocky islands at the foot of South America and sailed through into the Pacific Ocean. After months of hardship, hunger and thirst, Magellan reached the Phillipine Islands, where he was killed in a battle between natives. Another officer took command of the survivors, who eventually sailed round the Cape of Good Hope and arrived back home, three years after they had set out. They were the first men ever to sail round the world.

During Elizabeth's reign there were many adventurous seamen who were eager to explore the seas. Many hoped to return with gold and silver from the mines in South America.

The most famous English seaman was Francis Drake who, in 1577, sailed the same route as Magellan through his Straits into the Pacific. There he planned to rob Spanish ships of the treasure they were taking back to Spain. One Spanish ship after another was surprised by Drake and his ship, the *Golden Hind*, became laden with gold and silver bars, jewels, silks and linen. When the ship could carry no more, Drake set sail for home across the Pacific and Indian Oceans, round the Cape of Good Hope and back to Plymouth. He was the first Englishman to sail round the world and Elizabeth knighted him for his bravery. Englishmen thought him a hero, but the Spanish called him a pirate.

Sir Walter Raleigh, who attempted to form an English colony in America. He called it Virginia. His seamen brought tobacco and potatoes back to England. When he displeased Queen Elizabeth, she sent him to the Tower of London. Later, he was released, but during the reign of James I he was again sent to the Tower and after 13 years, beheaded.

Drake's 'Golden Hind'

Defeat of the Spanish Armada

King Philip of Spain, who had been the husband of Mary I, believed he should be King of England. Drake and other English seamen had annoyed him by robbing his Spanish ships. So, in 1588, he prepared to invade England and gathered together a great fleet of ships, or Armada. The Spanish planned to sail up the English Channel and take aboard a large army of soldiers at Calais. Then they would sail across the Channel and land them on the English coast.

Most of the English fleet with Drake and Hawkins was at Plymouth, where it was thought the Spanish would invade. At the first sight of the approaching Armada, warning beacon fires were lit and the news blazed from hilltop to hilltop across the country. People prepared to defend their homes and the English fleet, under Admiral Lord Howard, sailed out to attack the Spanish Armada. Fierce battles were fought off the Isle of Wight, but the Spanish ships were massed closely together and despite some damage, sailed on towards Calais. There they anchored to await the arrival of the Spanish soldiers.

During the night, 8 old English ships, filled with barrels of tar and gunpowder, were towed towards the Spanish fleet. At a signal they were set alight and the Armada scattered to avoid the blazing ships. A fierce battle followed and the battered Spanish ships, now short of ammunition and food, escaped northwards round the coasts of Scotland and Ireland. But severe storms drove many of the damaged ships on to the rocks and less than half of the Armada returned to Spain.

Weapons and armour

Pikes were long and were carried by the tallest and strongest men. The pikemen held off the enemy and protected the musketeer as he loaded his musket.

In early Tudor times there was no real army, but every Englishman between 16 and 60 could be called upon to defend his country. They had no uniform, but a few had a coat of armour and most of them wore a leather jerkin. They had compulsory weapon training and archery practice.

During the reign of Mary, the 'militia', as it was called, was reorganised so that an army of 300,000 men could be called upon in time of emergency, though only about 30,000 were kept in training. Every village and town had to provide armour, pikes, muskets and longbows in time of war.

When gunpowder was invented, it was used first for the firing of cannons, but later it led to the use of muskets. Gradually firearms replaced the longbows.

The musket was a slow and clumsy weapon to use. The musketeer loaded it by ramming gunpowder down the barrel, followed by a stone or lead bullet. It was fired by placing a glowing piece of cord, called a match, against a pinch of gunpowder at the rear of the barrel. The musketeer carried a flask of powder, a spare match, a bag of bullets, a rest to support the barrel of the musket when firing and a sword.

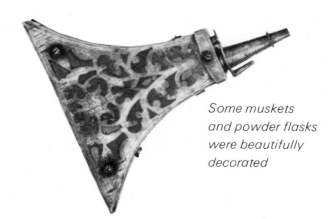

Some muskets and powder flasks were beautifully decorated

Look at this picture of a soldier firing a cannon. He is standing well back as he touches the gunpowder with his match! Notice the cannon ball leaving the mouth of the cannon as the gunpowder explodes.

Cannons were becoming larger and heavier and were mainly used for attacking walled towns and in sea battles. They were quite frightening weapons to fire, for the exploding gunpowder was both deafening and dangerous.

Armour was now lighter than that worn earlier and was not much use against cannon fire, though it could stop a musket bullet.

But many noblemen still had suits of armour made for tournaments, state occasions and in case of war. They sent their measurements to the armourer's workshop, where the armour was made and put together, piece by piece, like a suit of clothes. Those pieces which covered the man's head and chest were made thicker than the rest of the armour, to give extra protection where there was more risk of serious injury. Some workshops made cheaper armour for the ordinary soldiers.

Imagine how heavy and uncomfortable it was to wear, for a suit of armour usually weighed about 40 kilogrammes. Because of this, some soldiers began to leave it off and by the end of the 17th century, only cavalry wore any armour.

This suit of armour was made for Henry VIII at the armouries at Greenwich. It can be seen in the Tower of London.

Tudor clothes

During Tudor times the wealthier people's clothes were very elaborate and colourful. Ladies and gentlemen who attended the royal court and those who wanted to appear fashionable, spent large sums of money on their clothes.

These fashionable men's clothes can be seen in the Museum of London. Elizabethan ladies liked to work embroidery and the designs on cloaks, gloves and other garments were first drawn by an artist. Sometimes the embroidery was worked in silver and gold thread.

Man's leather hat, cloak and embroidered gloves

Here is a miniature portrait of an Elizabethan gentleman. Most gentlemen wore a tight-fitting tunic called a doublet, padded breeches and long stockings or hose. Sometimes the doublet and breeches were 'slashed' to show the brightly coloured linings underneath.

A Tudor workman with his paring spade

Ladies wore tight-waisted dresses of velvet or silk which were sometimes decorated with small jewels. By Elizabethan times, their skirts stuck out around them, as they wore a whalebone framework, called a farthingale, underneath them.

Collars of starched lace called ruffs, were worn by both ladies and gentlemen.

There were many laws concerning clothes which could be worn. Ordinary people were not allowed to dress like the nobles, but the rich merchants' long gowns were sometimes lined or trimmed with fur. Citizens' wives had to wear white knitted caps unless their husbands could prove themselves to be gentlemen by birth.

London apprentices wore flat woollen caps, blue gowns, white breeches and were not allowed to wear ruffs or jewellery.

One law said that woollen caps were to be worn on Sundays and Holy Days, by men and boys of 6 years and upwards, to help the wool trade.

This little girl, aged 4, lived at the time of Queen Elizabeth. Notice the ruff around her neck. Children were dressed like grown-ups.

This lady was maid of honour to Queen Elizabeth. Miniatures like this were worn as lockets or pendants.

Some Londoners wore caps like this. John Stow, a writer of the time, said they were 'so light they were forced to tie them under their chins, for else the wind would be master over them'. What did he mean?

The poorer people's clothes were made at home of rough, woollen cloth, or of a coarse, cotton material called fustian. There are very few still to be seen, for they were patched, repaired and worn until they were only fit for rags.

Peasants or workmen usually wore a jerkin over a shirt and breeches, but better off farmers sometimes had a leather doublet and wore a cloak when it was bad weather.

Games and entertainments

Look at the hunting scene on this piece of Elizabethan embroidery, which is part of a linen tablecloth.
Find:
—the huntsman with his hounds
—the water-mill and the windmill
—the farm worker carrying on with his job.
Notice the men's clothes. What else can you find in the picture?

Hunting for deer, wild boar and foxes was a popular sport enjoyed by the royal family and the noble classes. The poor poached in the woods for rabbits and hares for extra food, though new laws tried to stop them from doing so.

People feasted, danced and made merry whenever they could on church festivals, feast days and other special times of the year, such as May Day and harvest time.

Boys and girls played many of the games we still play today, such as hide-and-seek, leap-frog and hopscotch, while men played bowls and a game like golf, called 'bandy-bar'.

Some sports were cruel. People enjoyed going to a bear garden, where they watched dogs attacking a bear which was tied to a post. The fight was stopped when the dogs were killed or when the bear was seriously injured. Cock-fighting was another cruel sport where two trained fighting cocks fought against each other until one of them was killed, or badly injured.

Football was played in the villages with no proper pitch or rules. It was a very rough game and many people were injured.

Archery was a favourite sport in Tudor times. All men were expected to practise in case of war.

The theatre

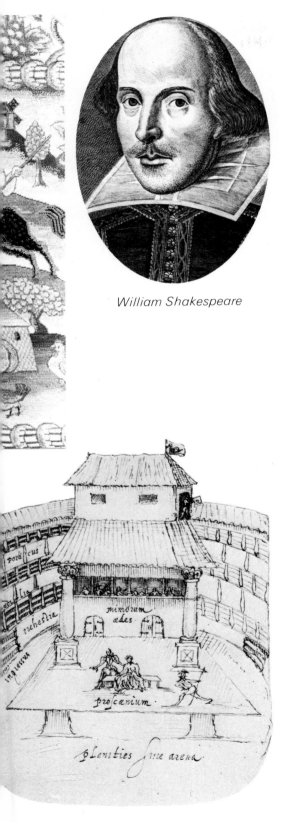

William Shakespeare

During the Middle Ages people had enjoyed watching the guilds act their biblical plays on wagons, or on temporary stages. In Tudor times other kinds of plays were acted by groups of players in the courtyards of large inns. People watched from upstairs windows or stood around the stage in the courtyard. The actors travelled from inn to inn, but many authorities considered them vagrants, for the only money they earned was from collections made in the inn yard.

During Elizabeth's reign the first theatres were built in London, outside the city walls. The City Aldermen did not approve of play-acting. Probably the most famous was *The Globe* theatre, where the plays of William Shakespeare were acted.

Here is an Elizabethan theatre called *The Swan*. Notice:
—the platform stage which jutted out into the open arena where some of the audience sat or stood
—the circular galleries for the wealthy
—the doors at the back of the stage through which the actors made their entrances
—the balcony which could be used by the actors
—the tall building at the back which had storage space for costumes and was used as dressing rooms by the actors. All the parts were played by men for it was considered improper for women to appear on the stage.
—the flag which showed a play was being performed.

Things to do

1 Draw pictures and write notes in your book about:
   a) seamen and explorers
   b) the Spanish Armada
   c) weapons and armour
   d) games and entertainments.
2 Use books in your library to find out more about:
   a) John Hawkins
   b) Sir Walter Raleigh
   c) William Shakespeare.
3 Make a model of an Elizabethan theatre.
4 On a map of the world draw the voyages of:
   a) Christopher Columbus
   b) Vasco da Gama
   c) Sir Francis Drake
   d) Ferdinand Magellan.

Stuart Kings and Queens

When Elizabeth I died in 1603 her cousin, James Stuart, became **King James I (1603 to 1625)** of England. He was the son of Mary, Queen of Scots and was already King of Scotland. So now England and Scotland had the same king, though they were governed separately.

In 1611 a new translation of the Bible, called the Authorised Version, was published. But many people were not allowed to worship God in the way they wished. In 1620 some of these, called Puritans, who believed in simple worship and plain living, sailed across the Atlantic in a little ship called the *Mayflower* and settled in America. Later, they became known as the Pilgrim Fathers.

After James's death in 1625, his son became **Charles I (1625 to 1649)**. Charles quarrelled frequently with his Parliaments and for 11 years ruled without one. The quarrels led to civil war between the king's supporters, Royalists or Cavaliers, and Parliament's soldiers, known as Roundheads. After many battles the Royalists were defeated by the Roundheads, led by Oliver Cromwell. King Charles was brought to trial, sentenced to death and publicly executed in 1649.

The Commonwealth Protectorate (1649 to 1660). After the death of Charles I, England had no king and Oliver Cromwell ruled the country. He refused to become King, but was later called Lord Protector of the Commonwealth. Many of his followers were Puritans, who believed that all pleasure was wicked. Beautiful things in churches like crosses, statues, carvings and stained glass windows were destroyed. Theatres were closed and laws passed to forbid games, music and dancing on Sundays, when it was illegal even to go for a walk, except to church.

After Cromwell's death, the people wanted a king back on the throne again. Prince Charles, who had escaped from the country after the execution of his father, was invited to return from Holland to become **King Charles II (1660 to 1685)**.

During his reign the Puritans were persecuted. Many fled to America and others were put into prison. But many people liked Charles II for he loved pleasure and supported music, dancing and the theatre.

James II (1685 to 1688), the brother of Charles II, tried to make England a Roman Catholic country.

The Duke of Monmouth considered he had a better right to the throne. He led a rebellion against the King, in the west of England, but was defeated. James sent Judge Jeffreys to try those rebels who had been captured and imprisoned. Some of the rebels were sentenced to be hanged and many others were sent to the West Indies as slaves.

Parliament eventually invited James's daughter, Mary, together with her Dutch husband, William of Orange, to rule together as King and Queen. William landed at Brixham in Devon and James fled to France.

William and Mary (1689 to 1702) ruled together until Mary died in 1694. As Parliament had invited them to become King and Queen, it made sure they would not be able to rule as they liked. New laws were passed which limited the rulers' powers.

After Mary's death, William ruled by himself until he died in 1702.

After William died, Mary's sister became **Queen Anne (1702 to 1714)**. She was the last of the Stuart rulers. During her reign there lived one of England's greatest generals, John Churchill, Duke of Marlborough. His most famous victory was in 1704 when he defeated the French army at the Battle of Blenheim.

In 1707 England and Scotland were joined together as the United Kingdom. The two countries were then governed by the same Parliament and used the same coinage, weights and measures.

The Gunpowder Plot

During the 16th and 17th centuries, people were not always allowed to worship God in the way they wanted, as we can nowadays. Usually, the King, or Queen, expected everyone to be of the same religion as themselves. Those who were not, were persecuted and often imprisoned or put to death.

England had been a Protestant country under Queen Elizabeth. The Catholics hoped that when James I became King, he would change the religion of the country, as he was a Catholic. But James did not wish to do so and angered the Catholics by fining them if they did not attend Protestant services and stopping Catholic bishops from coming to England.

A number of Catholics planned to blow up the House of Lords when James came to open the new session of Parliament on 5th November 1605. The King and all his nobles would be killed.

The plotters attempted to tunnel through to the House of Lords from a building next door, but found the work too difficult. So they hired a cellar underneath the House of Lords and secretly brought in barrels of gunpowder, which they hid under coals and firewood. But one of the nobles was warned in a letter from a friend to stay away from the Opening of Parliament and the plot was discovered. The building was searched at night and Guy Fawkes, one of the plotters, was found in the cellar guarding the gunpowder. He was arrested, taken to the Tower and cruelly tortured to reveal the names of his fellow plotters. They were hunted down and some were killed. The rest, with Guy Fawkes, were brought to trial, sentenced to death and executed.

Guy Fawkes's lantern. This can be seen in the Ashmolean Museum at Oxford.

This is a receipt for 36 barrels of gunpowder taken from the cellar beneath 'Parliament House' on 6th November 1605. Can you think why they had been put there?

The barrels were taken to the Tower of London armoury, where weapons, ammunition and gunpowder were stored for the defence of the city.

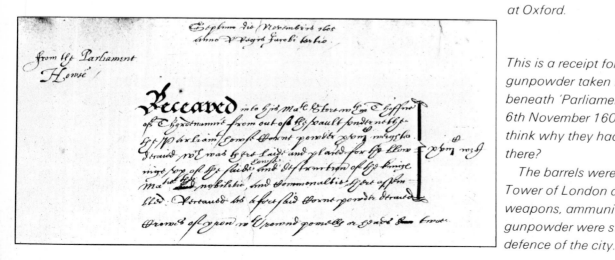

30

Civil War

When Charles I became King, he believed he had been chosen by God to rule the people by himself. But many Members of Parliament thought it was the work of Parliament to make laws and raise money to govern the country. This dispute led to many quarrels between those who supported the King and those who supported Parliament.

The short hair worn by the many apprentices and Puritans among Parliament's supporters gave them the name of Roundheads. Others wore their hair long like the Royalists, who were called Cavaliers. The King's supporters included many nobles and landowners.

When the fighting started in 1642, towns, villages and even families took sides. Sometimes men found themselves fighting against their own fathers, brothers or friends. Such a war, fought between people in their own country, is called a civil war. Many ordinary people were not interested in the war and in some parts of the country there was no fighting at all.

At first, neither army had any uniform and men wore their ordinary clothes, so it was difficult to tell friend from foe in battle, especially when there was hand-to-hand fighting.

In the picture below you can see that some of the soldiers are wearing pieces of armour and others leather jerkins. What weapons are they using? Can you tell which are the Royalists?

Many battles were fought up and down the country and in the first few years of the war it seemed as if the Royalists were winning. This was mainly due to the fearless fighting of their cavalry, led by the King's nephew, Prince Rupert, who had come over from Germany to help his uncle.

One of the Roundheads officers, Oliver Cromwell, began to train and discipline his cavalry to become fine fighters. At a battle at Marston Moor, his Ironsides as they were called, were very successful. After this, a well-equipped and well-paid New Model Army of 22,000 men was recruited and trained.

The Royalists were heavily defeated at the Battle of Naseby in 1645. This proved to be the last major battle of the war and in May the following year, Charles surrendered. There was some further fighting until September 1648.

Charles was brought to trial at Westminster Hall in London. He was accused of causing civil war and the deaths of thousands of his people. He was found guilty and sentenced to death.

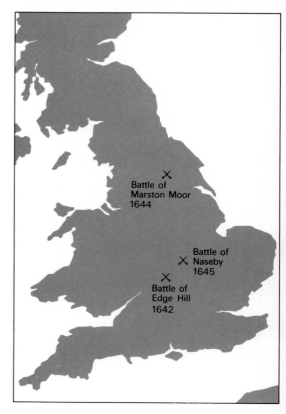

This map shows some of the major battles fought during the Civil War.

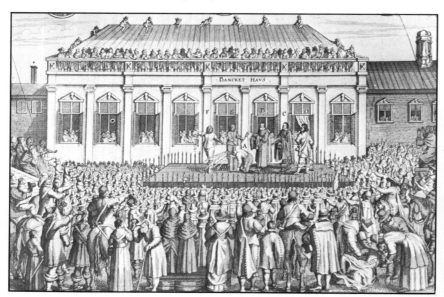

This picture shows the execution of Charles I in Whitehall, London, on 30th January 1649. He is the only English king ever to have been beheaded. Notice:
—the scaffold which had been built outside the Banqueting Hall of Charles's Palace in Whitehall
—the people watching from the windows and roof-top
—the rows of pikemen surrounding the scaffold
—the executioner with his axe
—the king kneeling at the block.
What else can you see in the picture?

Oliver Cromwell was a country gentleman and MP, who became a brilliant soldier. After Charles's death, he ruled the country, but refused to be crowned King.

Glassware and pottery

Few pieces of Elizabethan glass have survived over the years, as glass loses its brilliance after a while and eventually starts to flake.

This rare Elizabethan glass goblet was found stored in a hat box in a large country house and this probably protected it. It was sold recently for £75,000 at an auction in London. Can you see when it was made?

Most glass was brought from Venice, but some Venetian craftsmen settled in London.

This plate was made in honour of Elizabeth I, about 1600. It was probably made in Southwark, London, by Dutch potters who came over to England because of religious wars in Holland. Can you read the inscription around the picture in the centre?

This earthenware bottle is in the London Museum. Sack was a wine rather like sherry.

These delft mugs were made to celebrate the coronation of Charles II.

Stuart houses

In Stuart times, good timber for building houses became scarcer and although country people could still build wooden-framed houses, laws were passed to ensure that new houses in towns were built of brick and stone.

Blickling Hall, Norfolk

The timber frames of these small houses were filled with any local materials – bricks, stones, clay, mud or straw. The plaster patterns are called pargetting.

In the past, men had planned their own houses with the advice of local masons and carpenters. Now, if a man was rich enough, he could employ an architect to design his house for him.

One famous architect of Stuart times was Inigo Jones, who planned mansions and other buildings in the style of those he had seen when visiting Italy. These are sometimes called Palladian, after an Italian architect called Andrea Palladio.

Inigo Jones built the Banqueting Hall in Whitehall for James I. Can you remember what happened outside there in later years?

A stone house in Salisbury, Wiltshire

By the end of the Stuart period, smaller rectangular houses of an attractive style were being built, particularly in country towns. Here is one of them. Notice:
—the tiled roof which slopes down on all four sides and is called a 'hipped' roof
—the dormer windows in the roof
—the sash windows spaced equally on each side of the front entrance. These were opened by pushing half the window upwards or downwards.

Stuart furniture

During early Stuart times most furniture was still solid, heavy and made of oak. The poorer people's cottages were barely furnished, but in the houses of the better off craftsmen and farmers there were usually stools and benches, a long table and a chair for the head of the household, or a guest. Clothes and household goods were stored in chests.

The larger houses in town and country needed much more furniture. Servants no longer had their meals with the rest of the household at a long heavy table in the hall. People dined on smaller tables which had folding tops. These became known as gate-leg tables.

Furniture gradually became more comfortable and varied in design. Some chairs had cushions, or were padded with horsehair or wool and covered with tapestry or velvet. Later, chairs had cane or rush seats and backs.

Much of the new furniture was made of walnut instead of oak and chairs, stools and cabinets became lighter and more attractively designed.

In wealthier households the four-poster bed, with its carved headboard, elaborate canopy and beautiful hangings, was still the most valuable piece of furniture.

The date on this armchair is 1633. The back is inlaid with a diamond pattern in lime wood.

This is called a day-bed and is made of cane. Cane furniture could be made cheaply and quickly.

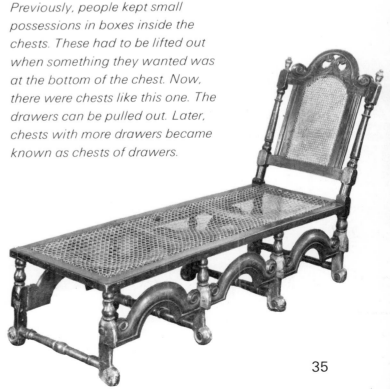

Previously, people kept small possessions in boxes inside the chests. These had to be lifted out when something they wanted was at the bottom of the chest. Now, there were chests like this one. The drawers can be pulled out. Later, chests with more drawers became known as chests of drawers.

35

Witches

During the 16th and 17th centuries almost everyone believed in witches and took various precautions to protect themselves against them.

Sometimes, stoneware witch bottles, containing human hair, nail-clippings, brass pins and iron nails, were buried under the hearthstone. It was believed they would protect the house. Any witch attempting to cast a spell on the occupants, would be trapped inside the bottle and suffer pain, or even death. This belief was most common in East Anglia and this bottle was discovered when a cottage was demolished near Ipswich.

A witch-bottle

Some people buried shoes, chickens or other birds in the walls when building Tudor and Stuart houses. They thought they would keep away evil spirits.

It was believed that witches could injure or kill people and animals, damage crops and bring on storms and lightning. Every witch was supposed to have a 'familiar', such as a cat or toad, which could be turned into a devil to do her work. Many an old lady living by herself with a cat was under suspicion.

In 1644, during the Civil War, Parliament instructed Matthew Hopkins of Manningtree to discover and bring to trial the large number of witches thought to be in the eastern counties. He was paid 20 shillings (£1) for each town he visited. Hundreds of people were arrested and tortured to make them confess.

This picture shows the 'trial' of one who failed to confess. The thumbs and toes of the suspected witch were tied together and she was then thrown into the nearest deep water. If she sank she was believed to be innocent, but if she floated she was thought guilty and hanged.

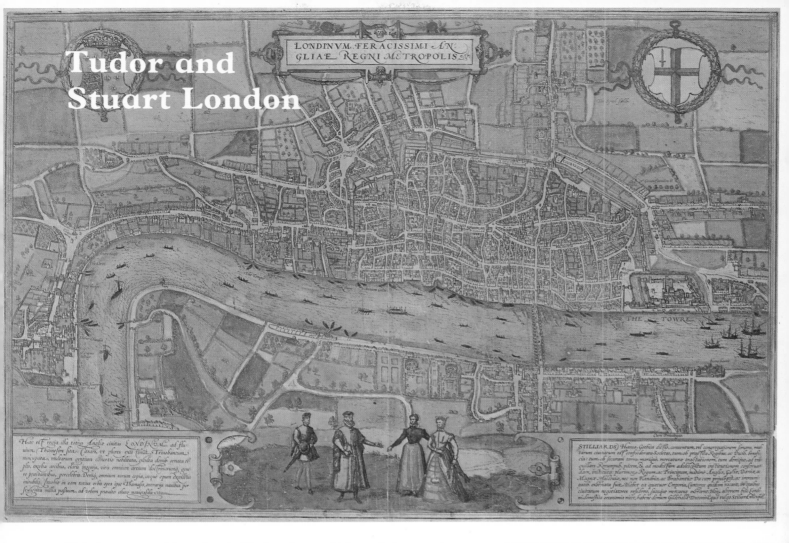

Tudor and Stuart London

LONDINVM FERACISSIMI ANGLIAE REGNI METROPOLIS

This is a map of London in Tudor times. Although it was the largest town in England, it was a very small place compared with London nowadays.

Look carefully at the map and find:

—the Tower of London on the right of the picture
—the Palace of Whitehall in the bottom left-hand corner
—parts of the wall which curved round three sides of the city. It stretched from the Tower to the Fleet Ditch which flowed into the River Thames.
—the gates in the wall, which were the main entrances to the city
—the densely crowded area within the wall. This was most of the city. Later, more houses were built outside the wall and along the river bank towards the separate city of Westminster. The two cities were eventually joined together.
—London Bridge across the river, to the village of Southwark
—the fields outside the wall. Many places which are now part of London were then villages in the country.

This model shows London Bridge in Tudor times. It was the only bridge across the river. It had houses and shops on both sides. At the Southwark end of the bridge heads of executed criminals were fixed on poles.

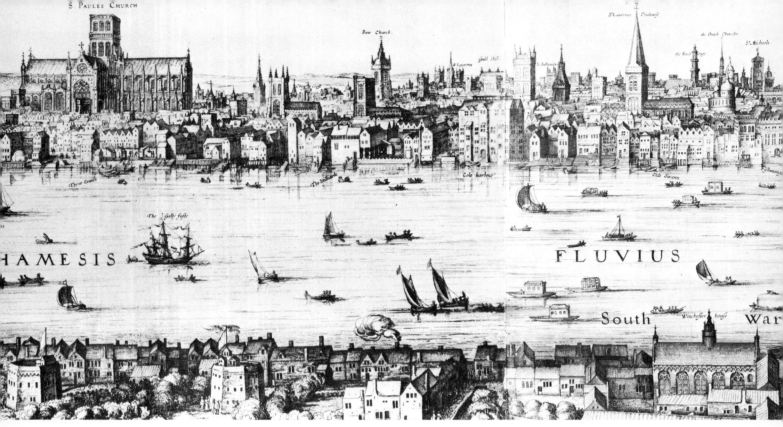

Look carefully at this picture of London about the year 1600. Notice the spires and towers of the many churches. There were over a hundred in the city at that time. Look at the large church of St. Paul's on the left of the picture. Its spire was struck by lightning soon after Elizabeth I became Queen and was never replaced, but you can see the square tower which remained. St. Paul's was used as a meeting-place for merchants as well as a place of worship. The nave was known as Paul's Walk and people went there to meet and talk with their friends, or to do business.

St. Paul's Churchyard was famous for its many bookstalls, with such names as *The Green Dragon, The Fox* and *The Angel.* Not far from St. Paul's was the Guildhall where the Lord Mayor, Aldermen and Council governed the city.

Look at the closely-packed houses along the bank of the river. Not all houses were as large as these. Most citizens lived in small, timber-framed houses, huddled together in narrow, winding streets. Many houses became overcrowded as more and more people came to live in the city, for there was no room for further building within the city walls. Horses and wagons clattered and rumbled over the cobbled streets, which were dirty, smelly and noisy. Few had any pavements. Often stalls were set out in the streets.

These people are listening to a sermon being preached at Paul's Cross—an open air pulpit in the middle of St. Paul's Churchyard. The defeat of the Spanish Armada was announced to the people of London from this pulpit.

Now find the small ferry boats with their passengers. Most people found it quicker and more pleasant to travel along the river. They walked down the steps to one of the many landing stages and called for a waterman to row them further along the river, or across to the south bank. Some people were frightened of the watermen, many of whom were rough, hard-swearing men, but they felt safer on the river than they did on the streets.

Queen Elizabeth often travelled along the river, too, in her gilded and painted barge. This was pulled along by another boat which was rowed by the Royal Watermen.

Notice the many sailing ships on the river. Some had brought goods from countries across the seas to the many warehouses, wharves and quays along the river bank. London was now a busy port and an important trading centre.

Now look for the Tower of London, on the right of the picture. This grim, stone castle was a royal palace and a mint where coins were made, but it was most feared as a prison. Traitors found guilty of treason, were brought down the river and through the entrance known as Traitors' Gate. Most of them were executed soon afterwards. Others were imprisoned there for many years.

Watermen ferrying passengers across the river. Notice the many arches of London Bridge. Sometimes the water rushed so swiftly downstream that small boats were overturned.

39

In early Tudor times London merchants had no building of their own in which to meet and do their business. Sometimes they met in the nave of St. Paul's and at other times in taverns, or in the open air. Trade with other countries was increasing and the merchants needed somewhere to carry out their business deals.

Eventually, a wealthy merchant called Sir Thomas Gresham paid for a hall to be built in Cornhill and after a visit by Queen Elizabeth in 1571 it became known as the Royal Exchange. It was built round a courtyard with arcades on each side, where English and foreign merchants could meet one another and do business.

The upper floor above the arcades was called the pawn, where there were fashionable shops selling luxury goods such as embroidered linens, porcelain and watches. The City Council ordered all goods to be made and sold in daylight, not by candlelight, to prevent poor workmanship and fraud. But many of the shops remained empty for the rents were too expensive. The pawn was also used as a place for recreation, where music was played and merchants walked in the evenings with their families and friends.

This shoe horn was made by Robert Mindum who kept a horner's shop upstairs in the Royal Exchange.

This model of the Royal Exchange can be seen in the Museum of London. Notice the entrance through to the arcades and the clock and bell on the tall belfry tower.

The Plague

Here is a model of the Fleet River, which flowed alongside the city wall into the Thames. Although at one time the Fleet had been kept clean, by the end of Elizabeth's reign it was choked with every kind of rubbish.

Look at Bridewell Palace on the left of the picture. This was built by Henry VIII to accommodate Emperor Charles V when he visited London. But the palace was too close to the foul-smelling river and dirty streets and was later given by Edward VI to the city as a workhouse.

Most Londoners still threw their refuse in the river and streets. The City Council realised this helped to spread disease. Orders were made for the sweeping of streets and the collection of rubbish.

The most feared disease in Tudor and Stuart times was the plague, for it was very infectious and nearly all who caught it died.

There had been outbreaks of plague since the Black Death in the Middle Ages, but no-one really knew what caused it. Many years later, it was thought the disease was caught from fleas carried on the many black rats which swarmed ashore from ships in the port of London.

Various orders were made to try to protect people's health during an outbreak of the plague.

> ### Care to be had of unwholfome Fiſh or Fleſh, and of muſty Corne.
>
> THat ſpeciall care be taken, that no ſtinking Fiſh, or unwholſome Fleſh, or muſtie Corne, or other corrupt fruits of what ſort ſoever, be ſuffered to bee fold about the City or any part of the ſame.
>
> That the Brewers and Tipling houſes be looked unto, for muſtie and unwholſome Cask.
>
> That order be taken, that no Hogs, Dogs, or Cats, or tame Pigeons, or Conies bee ſuffered to bee kept within any part of the City, or any Swine to bee, or ſtray in the Streets or Lanes, but that ſuch Swine bee impounded by the Beadle or any other Officer, and the Owner puniſhed according to the Act of Common-councell, and that the Dogs bee killed by the Dog-killers appointed for that purpoſe.

Can you read this? It will help if you remember that the letter 's' was written as 'f'.

No-one knew how to cure the plague though many strange remedies were tried.

This apothecary's jar and the small phials, or bottles, contained such medicines as powdered horn in water, alchohol and 'London treacle', which was a mixture of oil, gunpowder and sack.

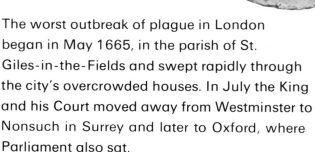

The worst outbreak of plague in London began in May 1665, in the parish of St. Giles-in-the-Fields and swept rapidly through the city's overcrowded houses. In July the King and his Court moved away from Westminster to Nonsuch in Surrey and later to Oxford, where Parliament also sat.

During the hot summer months the number of deaths increased and people began to leave the city, taking their possessions with them, for they were terrified of catching the plague. You can see some of them in this picture.

Soon only the very poor, the sick and the dying were left behind and London became a silent city. Shops closed down and all trading stopped. Nearly every occupied house had someone sick inside. There were no street cries, no rattling coaches and no clattering hooves on the cobble-stones. The streets were almost deserted except for watchmen and women searchers, who were paid a groat (fourpence) for each body they examined to find the cause of death. Sometimes the dog killer could be seen. He was paid twopence for each cat or dog he killed as it was thought they spread infection.

The people are leaving London by coach, by wagon, on horseback and on foot. Find the man who is showing his certificate of health to the guards as he approaches a nearby town. This certified he was free from the plague.

In September the plague was at its worst and thousands of people were dying each week. Look at this picture of a London street at night.

Notice:

—the parish burial cart which came round each night to collect the bodies of those who had died during the day

—the driver with his handbell. This, with his cry of 'Bring out your dead!', warned people of his approach.

—the plague-stricken houses whose doors were marked with a red cross to warn people to keep away. The doors were locked and bolted and the windows shuttered until forty days after the sick person inside had died or been cured.

—the watchman who guarded the closed houses to prevent anyone from entering or leaving. But some managed to escape, spreading the disease wherever they went. Those who could not, faced almost certain death in the house.

As the cold winter months approached, the infectious germs did not spread so rapidly and the plague began to die down. Slowly, people began to return and gradually the city came back to life. Shops re-opened and people began to walk the streets again.

By March 1666, the plague was practically over. Almost 100,000 people had died in London and thousands more in other parts of the country.

These burial carts are bringing their loads outside the city walls. Huge burial pits were dug, because the churchyards were full.

This handbell, used by the driver of a burial cart, can be seen in the Museum of London.

The Great Fire of London

This is a picture of the Great Fire of London which struck the city only a few months after the plague died down. It began in a baker's shop in Pudding Lane in the early hours of Sunday 2nd September 1666 and a strong east wind blew sparks from the blazing building to the stables of an inn in nearby Fish Street Hill. Soon the hay and straw in the stable yard were alight and the fire spread quickly to the inn itself and to nearby buildings.

The great sheds and warehouses near the river, with their inflammable contents of cheese, wine, oil, tar, timber and other goods, were next ablaze. The fire raced rapidly through the narrow streets destroying houses, inns and churches. Even St. Paul's Cathedral and the Guildhall went up in flames.

Samuel Pepys, who kept a diary at that time, wrote: 'I did see the houses at the end of the bridge all on fire.' The long gap beyond the burning houses prevented the fires from spreading further along London Bridge, but people were unable to escape from the city across it.

Pepys went to see the King at Westminster, who commanded the Lord Mayor to pull down houses to clear spaces in front of the approaching flames.

Syringes, leather helmets and buckets like these were used when fighting the fire. They were provided by each parish and were usually kept in the church.

44

Now look carefully at the picture and find:
—the people forming a human chain of buckets and throwing water on the flames
—others using a hand syringe to try to put out the fires. A syringe squirted about a gallon of water.
—the team of men (with a horse) pulling down houses with long fire hooks and ropes
—the people trying to clear away the piles of thatch, timber and plaster before the fire reaches them
—the people carrying bundles of possessions along the street towards the river. Many stayed in their houses until the flames reached them.

—the handcart piled high with pieces of furniture and other belongings
—ferrymen rowing the crowded boats further up the river away from the flames, or across to the other side.

After the fire had burned for four days and nights, further orders were given for houses to be blown up by gunpowder. People were frightened when they heard the noise of the explosions, but larger gaps were made between the buildings and the flames were unable to cross them. Gradually the fires died down and by Thursday 6th September, they had practically burned themselves out.

The fire destroyed over 13,000 houses, 84 churches and many public buildings. Although very few people lost their lives, thousands were left homeless and camped out in the fields outside the city walls. Fortunately, the weather was fine.

When they returned later to the city, they found their homes reduced to heaps of ashes and smoking rubbish. John Evelyn, another diarist of the day, wrote:

'I clambered over mountains of smouldering rubbish . . . and the ground under my feet so hot that it ever hurt the soles of my feet.'

This is a receipt for money collected to help those who had suffered loss in the fire.
Many had lost all their possessions and had no money to replace them.

Here is part of an Act of Parliament which was passed in 1668 to prevent such a serious fire from happening again. It will help you to read it if you remember that the letter 's' was written as 'f'
Notice the city has been divided into 4 parts. Each part now had to have 800 buckets, 50 ladders, 2 water syringes and 40 large shovels.

The new St. Paul's Cathedral was designed by Sir Christopher Wren, a famous architect. He also planned many fine new churches, such as St. Bride's in Fleet Street and St. Mary-le-Bow in Cheapside.

People now realised the danger of living in timber houses built so closely together. Several plans were put forward for the rebuilding of the damaged city, with new wide streets, but most were thought too costly. So only a few streets were widened and most houses were rebuilt where they had stood before. But Charles II ordered that all new buildings were to be built of brick and stone.

The dirty, plague-infested houses had been destroyed and in their place a new and cleaner city arose out of the ashes. Today, the Monument stands within a few yards of the baker's shop where the Great Fire first started.

Frost Fairs

During very severe winters in Stuart times the Thames was frozen over on several occasions and fairs were held on the ice. There were booths, or stalls, selling hot spiced drinks, gingerbread and all kinds of things. There were also puppet plays, bull-baiting and other entertainments. Sometimes the ice was so thick that fires were lit and meat roasted.

In 1684 John Evelyn wrote:
'I went across the ice, now become so thick as to bear not only streets of booths, in which they roasted meat ... and shops of wares as in a town, but coaches, carts and horses passed over.' Look carefully at the picture and try to find the things John Evelyn wrote about. What else can you see in the picture?

Things to do

1 Draw pictures and write notes in your book about:
   a) the Civil War
   b) Stuart houses and furniture
   c) Tudor and Stuart London
   d) the Plague.
2 Make a model of London Bridge.
3 Paint large wall pictures of:
   a) Cavaliers fighting Roundheads
   b) the Great Fire of London
   c) a Frost Fair.

4 Imagine you lived in London in 1666 and write your story of the Great Fire. Tell how you were awakened by the smell of smoke and the crackling of flames. Write how you gathered together your possessions, what you saw and heard in the streets and what happened to you after you escaped.
5 Use books in your library to find out about:
   a) Stuart kings and queens
   b) Samuel Pepys
   c) Sir Christopher Wren.

Stuart clothes

During Stuart times there were many changes in fashions but, of course, not everyone dressed alike.

The Cavaliers wore brightly coloured clothes with lace collars instead of the Elizabethan ruffs. Most of them wore their hair long.

Ladies no longer wore the farthingale and their wide, high-waisted skirts were often looped up and worn over many petticoats.

A Puritan family. The Puritans thought it wicked to wear bright colours and their clothes were made of dark materials with plain, white, starched collars and cuffs. The men wore tall, black hats and the women small linen caps.

A Stuart gentleman. Notice his doeskin coat.

This lady's linen jacket is embroidered with silver and gold threads and has a lace collar.

This lady's embroidered linen cap was called a coif.

After Charles II became King, men's clothes changed considerably. Men began to wear coats and waistcoats instead of doublets. They were often decorated with embroidery and bows or loops of ribbon and velvet. They wore silk stockings and their shoes had metal buckles or bows of ribbon. Some gentlemen wore long curled wigs, which hung over their shoulders and almost down to the waist.

These fine clothes were only worn by the rich. Country people and the poorer townsfolk still wove their own material and made simple clothes for themselves. The women wore plain woollen dresses and the men breeches of wool or thin leather. Their clothes were still patched and repaired until they were no longer fit to be worn.

Georgian Kings

Four of the kings who ruled Britain from 1714 to 1837 were called George. So this time in our history has become known as Georgian.

When Anne died, George of Hanover became **George I (1714 to 1727)**. He spoke little English and spent little time in England. However, most people wanted him as king for he was a Protestant, whereas James II's son, James Edward Stuart, who fled to France, was a Catholic. Some of James's Scottish supporters tried to invade England, but failed.

During the reign of **George II (1727 to 1760)**, son of George I, the Stuarts made another attempt to claim the throne. The invasion was led by James's son, Charles ('Bonnie Prince Charles). Although they defeated an English army at Prestonpans and marched as far as Derby, they were defeated at Culloden. Charles escaped to France, disguised as a maid.

George III (1760 to 1820) was the son of George II. During his reign the settlers in America objected to paying taxes to Britain. Under George Washington, they fought the British for their independence and formed the United States of America. George III became a very sick man and his son, George, ruled for the last 9 years as Prince Regent.

After his father's death in 1820, the Prince Regent became **George IV (1820 to 1830)**. He was not a popular king and is best remembered for his fine collection of paintings and his seaside palace, the Royal Pavilion at Brighton.

William IV (1830 to 1837), right, was the brother of George IV and reigned for only 7 years.

Towns in Georgian times

A Georgian town house in London

At the beginning of Georgian times most people still lived in the country. Except for London towns were small, though some were larger than in Tudor times.

London had spread well beyond its city walls with a population of over half a million and was at least ten times larger than any other town in Britain. Norwich, which had become the centre of the East Anglian cloth trade, and Bristol, the main port in the west, were the next largest towns, but even these had less than 50,000 people.

Most other towns were really overgrown villages which had become market centres for the surrounding countryside. Any town with more than 5,000 people was considered large. But the population of Britain was increasing rapidly and great changes in the towns were on the way.

During the 18th century many people who had become wealthy through increased trade, moved out of the crowded town centres into fine new Georgian houses. These houses were built in a plain, simple style of red brick, sometimes faced with white plasterwork, known as stucco. They had equally spaced sash windows and graceful doorways. Some had dormer windows in the tiled roof.

Some Georgian houses were built separately and others in terraces or crescents. Sometimes these formed the sides of a square, with gardens and trees in the centre. Many were designed by a famous architect called John Nash. In London new districts, such as Mayfair, Regent's Park and Berkeley Square, became fashionable to live in, as did other towns such as York, Exeter and Chester.

right: A Georgian terrace at St. Leonard's Place, York

Here is the Royal Crescent, Bath, one of the beautiful terraces built by John Wood.

It was believed that springs and wells in certain towns contained mineral waters which could cure rheumatism and gout and also act as a tonic. There had been hot mineral springs at Bath since before Roman times and this now became the most fashionable town in England, except for London.

At first, people went there merely to drink the waters or bathe in them, but later it was considered important to be seen taking part in the busy social life of the town. Breakfast in the Assembly Rooms was followed by a visit to the Pump Room to 'take the waters'. After dinner, some shopping in the main streets and tea in the Assembly Rooms. The day finished with a ball or a visit to the theatre.

Bath was only a small town and new houses and other buildings were needed for the many fashionable visitors. Ralph Allen, Robert Adam, John Wood and his son, John, were some of the clever men who planned new streets and squares. They rebuilt much of the town in the elegant Georgian style, using the local honey-coloured stone.

Despite the fine houses and shops in the better areas, the poorer districts of London and other towns still had people living in overcrowded tenements and damp cellars. Others lived in wooden houses built with no proper foundations, drains, or water supply.

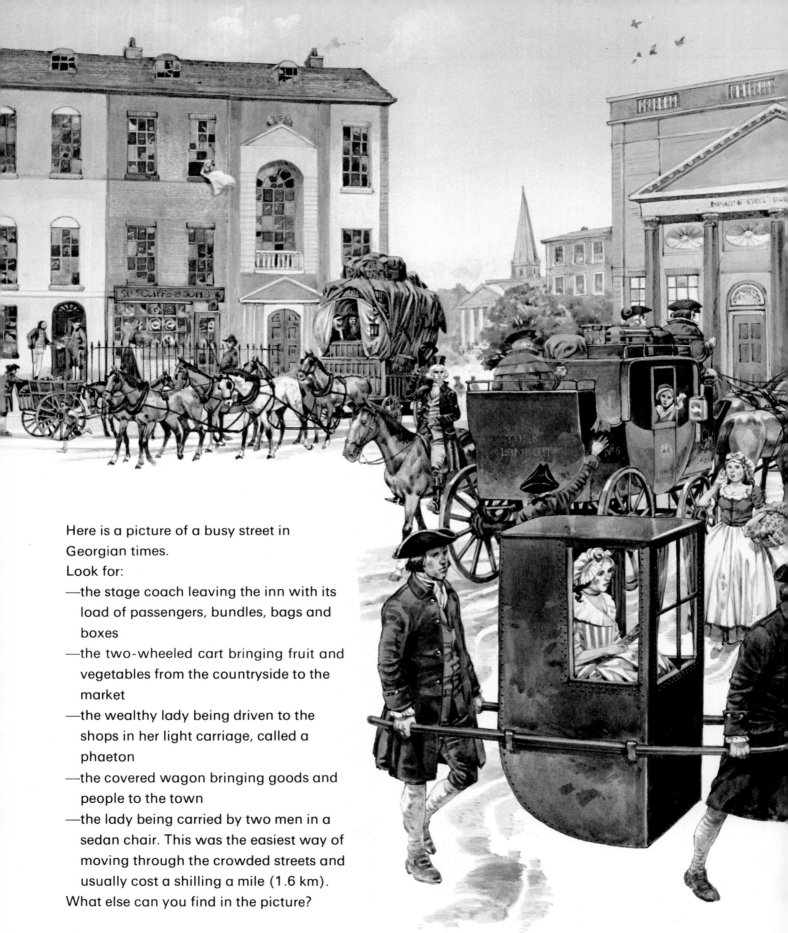

Here is a picture of a busy street in Georgian times.

Look for:

—the stage coach leaving the inn with its load of passengers, bundles, bags and boxes

—the two-wheeled cart bringing fruit and vegetables from the countryside to the market

—the wealthy lady being driven to the shops in her light carriage, called a phaeton

—the covered wagon bringing goods and people to the town

—the lady being carried by two men in a sedan chair. This was the easiest way of moving through the crowded streets and usually cost a shilling a mile (1.6 km).

What else can you find in the picture?

52

Here is a pewter shop which has been reconstructed in the Castle Museum at York. The large bow-fronted window came from Bath.

Look for the pewter plates, jugs and tankards. What else can you find in the shop window?

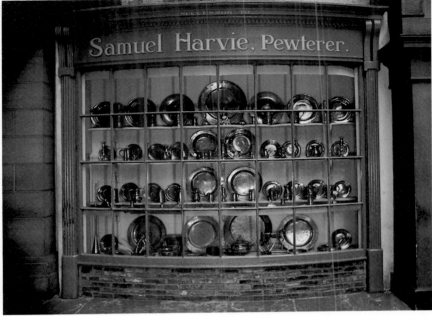

Samuel Harvie, Pewterer.

There were fewer shops in Georgian times than there are nowadays. Many goods were sold from stalls and barrows or by street sellers, who walked up and down shouting or singing their street cries. Cherries, oranges, eels, pies, oysters and hot gingerbread are only a few of the many things which were sold in this way. Here are some of the people at work in the busy streets.

The milkwoman

The dustman

The lamplighter

The knife-grinder

Entertainment

These are Vauxhall Gardens, which Londoners loved to visit. They were glad to leave the noisy, crowded streets and enjoy the fresh air and lovely surroundings. They could go down the river by boat from the new Westminster Bridge for a shilling (5p) and admission to the gardens cost them another shilling.

It was a fashionable place and families liked to dress up in their best clothes and mingle with the wealthier ladies and gentlemen as they walked across the lawns or under the trees. There were shady walks leading to groves and grottoes and there were pillars and statues, pavilions and lodges. There were stalls, too, where people could buy wines, tea and cold refreshments.

In one of the pavilions was a large round music room where people could listen to an orchestra playing and often there was dancing.

Sometimes, on special occasions, there was a balloon ascent or a display of fireworks in the gardens.

These men are gambling at one of the many clubs for wealthy gentlemen which were opened during Georgian times. Sometimes they gambled heavily all night at cards and lost large sums of money.

Another popular place for Londoners to visit along the river was Ranelagh Gardens. Here the admission price was half a crown (12½p), but this included tea, coffee and bread and butter, as well as a concert.

This is Astley's Riding School in Lambeth, where Londoners could watch daring riding displays and later, tumblers and clowns.

The concerts were held at this large circular building called the Rotunda. Sometimes people came there to walk with their friends and listen to the orchestra, or to sit at the tables under the balcony and have their refreshments. Often at night, dances were held there and the Rotunda was brilliantly lit by chandeliers of candles.

Country gentlemen came to London with their families for 'the Season' to visit the sights and join in the fashionable life of concerts, balls and the theatre. There were two big theatres in London at that time, the *Theatre Royal* at Drury Lane and the *Covent Garden Opera House*. Some of the audience sat in boxes alongside the stage, or even on the stage itself and the rest sat in the pit, the circle, or on uncomfortable seats high up in the gallery. Sometimes they threw orange peel at the actors if they did not like the performance.

Gentlemen spent a lot of their time at clubs and coffee houses, where they could drink coffee and meet and talk with their friends. Famous writers, poets, actors and artists all had their favourite coffee houses and other men went there to discuss with them politics, religion and other topics of the day. Many merchants carried out their business deals in the coffee houses, clubs and taverns.

Georgian clothes

This group of people are in the drawing room of a large Georgian country house. Notice the way they are dressed.

In Georgian times ladies wore long dresses like this, made of richly patterned materials. Their full skirts were usually stiffened with whalebone, or else stretched over hoops to make them stand out.

Ladies wore their hair in curls and ringlets. In later Georgian times they wore thickly powdered and curled wigs, piled up over small cushions into tall shapes. Sometimes they fastened imitation flowers or fruit on top!

The gentlemen in the picture are wearing tight-fitted tail coats, breeches and long, white stockings. One has lace cuffs, a cravat at his throat and is wearing a wig. Most gentlemen wore wigs and on special occasions these were perfumed, powdered and curled. Later on, a tax on powder stopped the fashion of powdered hair. In the morning, when at home, gentlemen often wore a nightcap or a turban over their close-shaven heads, instead of a wig.

Servants and working men wore their hair long, down to their shoulders. Children began to dress in their own styles of clothes, instead of being dressed by their parents to look like adults.

Some ladies wore lace caps on top of their hair.

Georgian country mansions

This fine Georgian mansion is Heveningham Hall in Suffolk. The park and gardens were landscaped by a gardener who was known as 'Capability' Brown, for he always said that an estate was 'capability of improvement'.

In Georgian times the noble and wealthy families owned huge estates of land and built stately country homes of stone and marble. Like Heveningham Hall, many had a large central block which was connected to a wing at each end by a colonnade, or gallery.

These great homes had impressive entrance halls and lofty rooms with beautifully decorated ceilings, fine paintings on the walls and elegant furniture.

Look at this dining room at Saltram House in Devon. It was designed by Robert Adam, a famous architect of that time.

Notice:
—the painted ceiling with its plaster decorations and pictures
—the framed paintings on the wall
—the white marble fireplace
—the dining table and chairs.

Georgian furniture

The large country mansions and town houses needed more furniture than had earlier homes. Trade with other countries brought fresh ideas and new woods to England and craftsmen began to design their own particular styles of furniture.

Walnut, beech and mahogany replaced the heavy oak of earlier times and the new elegant Georgian furniture was soon in great demand. A number of small towns became centres for furniture making. Cabinet makers made beautiful bookcases, chests of drawers and cabinets. Some had cleverly hidden secret compartments.

Three of the best known furniture designers of that time were Thomas Chippendale, George Hepplewhite and Thomas Sheraton. Here are some examples of their furniture.

A Chippendale cabinet. Thomas Chippendale had a cabinet-making workshop in London and made furniture for many wealthy people. He also published the first important book of furniture designs. He called it the 'Director'

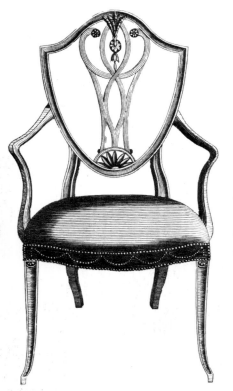

A mahogany 'shield' chair made by Hepplewhite

A Sheraton styled mahogany sideboard

New ways of farming

In this picture a villager is sowing seed broadcast. He is scattering the seed over the ground as he walks along. This way of sowing seed was slow and wasteful.

For hundreds of years life in the villages had not changed a great deal. Much of the land had been farmed in large open fields divided into strips. The fields had no hedges or fences and there were narrow grass banks, called balks, between the strips. The villagers had to decide the crops to be grown in each field and when they should be sown and harvested.

In Tudor times landowners had let some of their land as farms for rent and some farmers began to enclose their land by putting hedges and fences round it. Then they could farm the land how they liked.

Between 1700 and 1800 the population was growing and farmers needed to find better ways of farming to produce more food, particularly meat and corn.

In 1701 a farmer called Jethro Tull invented a machine which sowed the seed evenly in straight rows across the field. This enabled farm workers to weed and hoe between the rows and produce better crops. Other machines soon followed, including cast-iron ploughs and threshing machines.

A Norfolk landowner called Lord Townshend grew turnips and clover in the fields which had previously been left fallow every third year. These provided winter food for his cattle, which no longer had to be slaughtered in the autumn. Now people could eat fresh meat all the year round.

Other farmers, like Robert Bakewell of Leicestershire and Thomas Coke of Norfolk, began to raise better breeds of cattle and sheep, which produced greater quantities of meat.

Gradually, other farmers began to use the new farm machines and improved methods of farming. One man called Arthur Young travelled round the country on horseback and wrote a book about the different ways of farming he had seen.

A drill plough with seed and manure hoppers

Changes in the villages

The farmers now realised the new farming methods could be used only on enclosed land. So many wealthy farmers tried to buy more strips of land from the poorer villagers, who did not always want to sell them. But it was fairly simple for the farmers to get Parliament to pass laws, or Acts, to enclose the village land.

Here is the first page of an Enclosure Act. Notice the letter 's' is often written as 'f'. Read the document carefully and find out:
—the various kinds of land to be 'inclosed'
—the parish and county in which the land was situated
—the rector of the parish
—the lord of the manor.

The Enclosure Act was dated 12th May 1809. Can you find out who was king?

The Act states that 'all the land in the said Parish should be exonerated from Tythes'. Find out all you can about 'Tythes' and to whom they were paid.

When the Act had been passed, Parliament sent officers called commissioners to the village, to hold a public meeting and appoint surveyors.

AN

A C T

FOR

Inclofing Lands in the Parifh of *Barton-in-the-Clay*, in the County of *Bedford*.

WHEREAS there are in the Parifh of *Barton-in-the-Clay*, in the County of *Bedford*, divers Open and Common Fields, Common Paftures, and other Commonable and Wafte Lands: Preamble.

And whereas *Edward Willes*, Efquire, is Lord of the Manor of *Barton-in-the-Clay*, within the faid Parifh:

And whereas the King's Moft Excellent Majefty is Patron of the Rectory of *Barton-in-the-Clay* aforefaid; and the Reverend *John Hawkins*, Clerk, is Rector of the faid Parifh:

And, whereas the faid *Edward Willes*, *John Sowerby*, Efquire, *William Inglis* and *James Campbell*, Efquires, and divers other Perfons, are feverally the Proprietors of the faid Open and Common Fields, Common Paftures, and other Commonable and Wafte Lands, and are defirous that the fame fhould be divided, allotted and inclofed, and that all the Land in the faid Parifh fhould be exonerated from Tythes: BUT fuch Division, Allotment, Inclofure and Exoneration from Tythes cannot be effected without the Aid and Authority of Parliament;

May it therefore pleafe Your MAJESTY,

That it may be Enacted; And be it Enacted by the KING's Moft Excellent MAJESTY, by and with the Advice and Confent of the Lords

46.   A

In the picture on the left surveyors are measuring and mapping the land held by each person in the village. When the map was completed, the commissioners shared the land among those farmers and other villagers who could prove they owned it. Those who could not, lost their land.

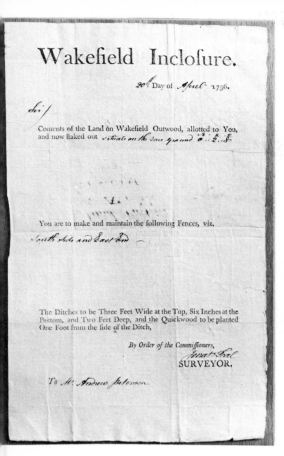

Wakefield Inclosure.

20ᵗ Day of April 1796.

Sir /

Contents of the Land on Wakefield Outwood, allotted to You, and now flaked out *situate on the law ground* ʼ0 .. 2 .. 8

You are to make and maintain the following Fences, viz.

South Side and East End —

The Ditches to be Three Feet Wide at the Top, Six Inches at the Bottom, and Two Feet Deep, and the Quickwood to be planted One Foot from the side of the Ditch,

By Order of the Commiffioners,
Great Seal
SURVEYOR.

To Mr Andrew Paterson

This document shows the fencing and ditching to be carried out following an enclosure of land at Wakefield in Yorkshire.

Many villagers could not afford the cost of enclosing or fencing their land, or the high legal fees payable to the lawyers and commissioners. So they were forced to sell their land to one of the richer farmers.

The Enclosure Acts ruined many of the poor villagers. Some were able to get work as labourers on the same land they had once owned, but fewer were needed because of the new farming methods. Those who did find work on the farms were very poorly paid and some earned as little as eight shillings (40p) a week.

Many who lost their land could no longer keep pigs, cows, or poultry, nor could they grow corn or many vegetables. They had to buy most of their food and prices were high.

This thatched cottage was built on common grazing ground by a villager who had no land of his own. He lived by keeping a few pigs, geese and chickens on the common land. Notice the roughly made wooden fence which kept cattle from straying on to the patch of land around his cottage.

When the common land was enclosed he was forced to leave and his cottage was pulled down. He had lost both his living and his home.

This special type of barn is called a granary and was used for storing grain. Notice the 'staddle stones' on which it stands. They prevent the damp from reaching the grain and rats and mice from getting inside the granary.

Many villagers poached game in the nearby woods to save their families from starvation. Gamekeepers patrolled the woods to protect the pheasants, partridges, rabbits and hares which were reared by wealthy landowners for their own sport.

Look at this picture. Poachers have been discovered by gamekeepers and a fight is in progress.
Notice:
– how the keepers are armed
– the clothes they are wearing
– the weapons the poachers
   are using.

Game Laws were passed which imposed severe penalties on poachers who were caught. They could be sentenced to imprisonment, a public whipping, transportation to a country overseas for seven years and even hanging if the keepers were violently attacked. No wonder the poachers in the picture are trying desperately to get away.

Some villagers who could get no work at all, went with their families to the parish poorhouse, where they lived in drab, dreary surroundings. Their meagre, plain diet barely kept them from starvation. Many villagers, rather than enter the poorhouse, left their parishes for the towns in the hope of finding work there.

Some landowners hid mantraps like this in the woods.
They could cruelly injure a poacher for life.
Can you see how it worked?

Each parish was responsible for the care of its own poor, and a poor rate was charged to every householder by officials called the Overseers of the Poor.

But there were many poor people who could not prove they belonged anywhere and could receive no help. So they were passed from parish to parish.

Look at this document which authorises the removal of Ellen Trowls from the parish of Hadleigh in Suffolk to the parish of Coggeshall in Essex. Find:

—who had asked for her removal and who had authorised it

—when the order was made.

Perhaps Ellen was moved on again after a few weeks in Coggeshall.

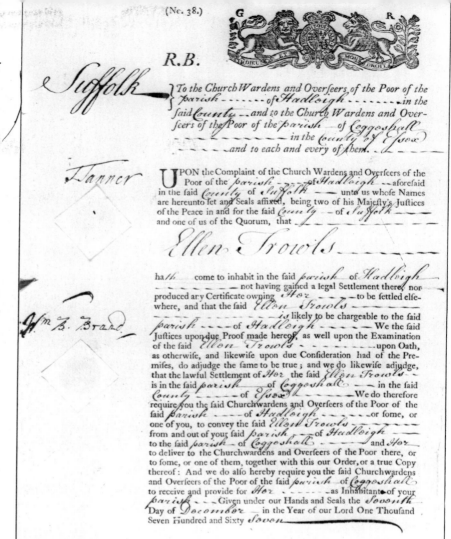

Things to do

1 Draw pictures and make notes in your book about:
   a) Georgian towns
   b) Georgian country mansions
   c) new ways of farming.

2 Paint a large wall-frieze of a street in Georgian times. Show the houses, the shops with their signs, a coaching inn and the different forms of transport. Make cardboard stand-up figures of the street sellers and other people in the street.

3 Use books in your library to find out more about Georgian kings.

4 Make a model in a large cardboard box of a Georgian dining room.

5 Make a wall chart about Georgian furniture. Include pictures of furniture by Chippendale, Hepplewhite and Sheraton. You may find examples of other Georgian furniture in books in your reference library.

6 Imagine you lived in a village where the land had been enclosed. Write a story telling how you went to the public meeting, how the surveyors came to measure up your strips of land and what happened to you afterwards.

Trafalgar

In 1805 England was threatened with invasion by France. Already the French leader, Napoleon Bonaparte, had conquered most of Europe and now he hoped to invade England. He gathered together a large army at Boulogne, but needed warships to protect his army as it made its way across the Channel to England.

At that time England had a famous admiral, Horatio Nelson, who had had a brilliant career. He had already won victories a few years earlier against the Spanish fleet off Cape St. Vincent, Portugal and the French fleet at the mouth of the River Nile.

On 21st October 1805, the French and Spanish fleets were sighted leaving Cadiz harbour on the west coast of Spain. Nelson prepared the British fleet for battle.

Look at this painting of a scene on Nelson's ship during the battle off Cape Trafalgar.

Notice:
—the gun crews firing their cannon
—the marines, who were soldiers on the ship, firing their muskets at the enemy's decks
—Nelson lying wounded on deck. He had been shot in the chest by a musket ball fired from a French ship.

By the time Nelson died a few hours later, the enemy ships had surrendered and England was no longer in danger of invasion. The British people were overjoyed at the victory at Trafalgar, but sad at the loss of their great leader. Nelson's body was brought back to England and buried at St. Paul's Cathedral.

This medal was made by Matthew Boulton, a Birmingham businessman, to remember Trafalgar.

This is Nelson's ship, 'The Victory', as it was at the Battle of Trafalgar. It can now be seen at Portsmouth Harbour.

Waterloo

Here is another battle against the French, which happened ten years after Trafalgar. Napoleon was still trying to conquer all Europe and England was helping her allies to fight against him.

The English leader was the Duke of Wellington, who had already won great victories against the French army in Spain and Portugal. After a further defeat at Toulouse in France, Napoleon surrendered and was sent to the Mediterranean island of Elba in April 1814. The following year he escaped, gathered his army together and invaded Belgium.

Wellington was put in charge of an army of Belgian, Dutch, German and British soldiers and decided to fight the French near the village of Waterloo. The battle started on the morning of 18th June 1815.

Now look closely at the painting above. It shows Wellington's soldiers being attacked by the French cavalry.

Notice:

—the front rows of Wellington's soldiers with their upturned bayonets. These formed a fence of sharp steel against the cavalry charge.

—the other soldiers firing their muskets

—the French cavalry charging with drawn swords

—the dead soldiers and horses and the broken cannon.

What else can you see in the picture?

As evening approached, Wellington ordered the British Guards into the attack. Their musket fire mowed down the front ranks of the French soldiers, who turned and fled as the British cavalry charged among them with drawn swords. The Battle of Waterloo was won and the long wars between the English and French had come to an end. England's two leaders, Nelson and Wellington, had brought peace and honour to their country. You can read more about these great men and of life in the navy and army in the *Focus on History* book called *At the Time of Nelson and Wellington*.

The Duke of Wellington

The coming of machines

Ever since the Middle Ages Britain's main industry had been the making of woollen cloth. Since about 1640, ships had been bringing raw cotton from India and cotton as well as woollen cloth was being made in some parts of the country.

But there were few machines or factories as we know them today. Most people still lived in villages and spinning, dyeing and weaving were carried out in the villagers' cottages

A weaver's cottage at Marsden, near Huddersfield

Here is a picture of some of the villagers at work. Two of the women are using spinning wheels, another is winding the thread into a 'skein' and the woman at the back of the room is mixing a dye over the fire to colour the thread. What else can you find in the picture?

The raw cotton or wool was brought to the villagers by merchants, who later returned to collect the woven cloth and pay the spinners and weavers for their work.

During the 18th century the population of Britain was growing fast and more goods were needed. But the workers were unable to make enough in their own cottages and workshops. So new machines were invented which speeded up spinning and weaving and enabled more cloth to be made by the same number of workers.

Here are two of the new machines. They can be seen at the Science Museum in London.

This 'spinning jenny', invented by James Hargreaves in 1767, could spin 8 threads at once. It was worked by turning the handle at the side.

This spinning frame, invented by Richard Arkwright in 1769, spun stronger threads than the 'spinning jenny'. The wheel was turned by a horse which walked round in a circle.

Soon it was discovered that the new machines could be driven by water power. The rushing streams tumbling down the slopes of the Pennines in Yorkshire, Lancashire and Derbyshire, were powerful enough to turn large water-wheels and these drove the machines. Large mills, or factories, were built along the river banks and people began to move into the towns and look for work in the new factories.

In 1712 Thomas Newcomen had invented a steam engine for pumping water out of mines, but although these were used throughout the 18th century, they were expensive to build, noisy to run and used as much as 13 tons (over 13,000 kg) of coal a day.

Several engineers tried to improve Newcomen's engines, but without success. Then, in 1781, a Scotsman called James Watt built an engine with financial help from a Birmingham businessman called Matthew Boulton. Watt's engine could rotate, or turn, a large fly-wheel. He made further improvements so that a belt could be attached to the fly-wheel to drive the machinery in the new factories.

Quarry Bank Mill, one of the early spinning mills worked by water power

An early steam-powered mill in Manchester

Watt's rotative engine at the Science Museum

Watt's rotative engines showed how steam could be used to drive all kinds of machinery. Factories were no longer dependent on water power and more factories began to be built near the coalfields, as coal was needed to fuel the steam engines.

Britain was changing from a rural to an industrial country and more and more people moved into the towns to look for work.

Iron and steel

This is a picture of the ironworks at Coalbrookdale in Shropshire in the 18th century. For hundreds of years, iron ore had been dug from the ground and smelted into iron by using charcoal. Charcoal is made from smouldering wood and so, until then, ironworks had been built close to wooded areas.

Large supplies of iron were needed to make the new engines and factory machinery and in the early 18th century Abraham Darby, at his Coalbrookdale works, discovered that iron could be made by using coal and coke, instead of charcoal.

Look again at the picture above.
Notice:
—the furnaces with their smoking chimneys, where iron ore was heated and melted to separate the metal from the rock
—the workshops in front of the furnaces where metal was re-melted, cast into moulds and shaped as required
—the cylinder for a new engine being carried away on a wagon by a team of horses.

As more iron was needed, foundries were built near the coalfields where large quantities of coal were close at hand. Birmingham, Sheffield and Newcastle became the country's main iron-manufacturing centres. In some areas, particularly around Sheffield, some of the iron was refined into steel and made into cutlery and various tools.

This iron bridge across the River Severn, near Coalbrookdale, was the first iron bridge in the world.

In the factories

Much of the work in the factories was done by women and children, so many factory owners arranged for children and young people to be sent to them from workhouses to work as apprentices. They paid them little and the parishes from where they came were glad to be rid of the expense of keeping them.

This document is an Indenture, or agreement, in which a cotton manufacturer agreed to train one of these children, called Thomas Jones, to be a cotton spinner. Read the document carefully and try to find the answers to these questions:

a) what was the year of the Indenture?

b) how old was Thomas?

c) who was to be his employer and where did he live?

d) how long was Thomas to serve him?

e) what did his employer promise to provide for him?

Children like Thomas lived crowded together in lodging houses near the mills. Their clothes were ragged and threadbare and they seldom had enough to eat. They worked at the factories from early morning until late at night and sometimes they were beaten to keep awake.

Girls at work in a factory

Not all children were from workhouses. Many were sent by their parents to earn a few pence to help the family. Some were only 4 or 5 years old. Many suffered serious accidents from the dangerous machinery.

People who had left the villages found that working in a factory was very different from working in a cottage. The hours were long, discipline was strict and workers were fined for all kinds of minor offences. One spinner in a cotton mill was fined a shilling (5p) for whistling and another was fined the same amount for being 5 minutes late for work. In those days, too, a shilling was almost a whole day's wage.

As the many factories were built, at first along the river banks and later in towns near the coalfields, the owners built houses to attract workers to work for them.

Look at this picture of the industrial part of Leeds during the Factory Age. Leeds was one of many towns where factories quickly sprang up following the invention of steam engines. Notice:
—the large factories with their tall chimneys
—the thick black smoke pouring out of many of the chimneys. Everywhere around the factories became very dirty.
—the houses jumbled together in the centre of the picture
—the street of terraced houses on the left.

below: Inside a small house, near a Leeds factory

Long rows of small back-to-back houses like these were built as cheaply as possible. They were poorly lit, badly ventilated and had no gardens or backyards. Several houses shared one outside toilet and water tap. Usually these were at the end of the row and often the water was turned on for only a few hours each day.

Most of the houses were overcrowded and unhealthy. Some families had only one room in which to live and hardly any furniture.

Down the mines

Before the invention of the steam engine,
horses had been used to turn wheels. At some
colliery pit-heads, they worked the winding gear
which carried miners to and from their work below
the ground and also brought coal to the surface.
James Watt's steam engines did this work
more efficiently.

Look at this colliery pit-head in Staffordshire. Notice:
—the steam engine in its tall engine house
—the globe-shaped boiler with the brick furnace underneath
—the loaded trolley being raised from the left-hand
   shaft. A man is pushing a trapdoor over the shaft so that
   the trolley can be lowered on to it and pushed along the
   railed track to one of the mounds of coal in the picture.
What else can you see in the picture?

Men, women and children worked long hours underground in
dangerous and unhealthy conditions. There was always the
risk of explosions, flooding, or falls of coal.
Trucks laden with coal were pulled along by
girls and boys who were unable to stand
upright in the low tunnels. Children, some
only five years old, spent long hours alone
in the darkness, opening and closing trapdoors
which controlled the flow of air in the mines.

A girl pulling a load of coal.

Roads

Since 1555 each parish had been responsible for the repair and upkeep of its own roads, but often these were little better than rough tracks and were full of deep holes and ruts. In bad weather the holes filled with water and the heavy wheels of carts and wagons churned up the mud and made the ruts deeper.

Look carefully at the picture above and notice:
—the surveyors who are organising the work. Two surveyors were chosen by the parish each year, but few of them knew much about roadmaking.
—the labourers throwing stones into the largest holes and filling ruts with earth. Most people in the parish had to work on the roads for 4 or 6 days each year, but sometimes they paid money to the parish for someone else to do the work for them.
—the travellers on the roads. Some have left the mud and are making a fresh track across the fields.

Eventually Parliament allowed money to be collected from people who used the roads. This money was spent on repairing them. Turnpikes and gates were set up across the busiest roads every few miles and tolls, or fees, were demanded for vehicles and animals, to pay for repairs to the roads.

Here is a tollgate on one of the main roads outside London. Notice:
— the gates across the road
— the tollhouse beside the gate
— the tollkeeper collecting tolls at the gate
— the coach and horses approaching the tollgate
— the covered wagon.

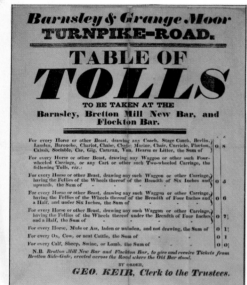

People did not always pay their tolls willingly, for they thought it unfair that some people and vehicles could pass through the gates without payment. There were frequent arguments at the tollgates and sometimes soldiers were called in to restore order.

Gradually some roads were improved, but others remained as bad as ever. The Ipswich Journal in 1769 reported what happened to one traveller:

'This day an inquest was taken at Ingatestone on the body of Richard Aimes when it appeared that the deceased was thrown from his horse . . . into a ditch and was suffocated by mud and filth.'

More and better roads were needed.

Fortunately, about this time certain men began to build new roads. The first was John Metcalf, known as Blind Jack. Despite his blindness, he built over 300 kilometres of roads in Yorkshire and Lancashire.

Another engineer, Thomas Telford, built many new roads and bridges. His roads were well drained and had a foundation of large stones with smaller stones rammed down on top.

James McAdam became the greatest roadmaker of that time. He thought deep foundations were unnecessary and built his roads with a layer of small hard stones which were pressed together by the traffic passing over them. The more his roads were used, the firmer they became.

Metcalf's measuring wheel. As he pushed it along, the dial measured the distance it travelled.

73

Coaches

The new roads enabled more people to travel about the country than before and stage-coaches ran regularly between most of the main towns. Some journeys lasted for several days. It took two days to travel from London to Norwich, four days to York and the long journey to Edinburgh lasted ten days. In bad winter weather the journeys often took much longer.

Each night the coaches stopped at an inn, where the passengers could have a meal and snatch a few hours sleep before starting off again early the next morning.

A coach timetable

Here a stage-coach has arrived at an inn.
Look at:
—the passengers getting down from the coach. They would be stiff and sore from their day's travelling, for the heavy coach had few springs and bumped and rattled along at about 10 kilometres an hour. There was room for 6 passengers inside the coach and others travelled on the roof for a much cheaper fare.
—the luggage in the basket slung at the rear of the coach. Sometimes a few passengers travelled in there.
—the ostler unharnessing the horses. He took them away to the stables to be fed and watered. Horses were changed about every 15 kilometres of the journey at inns which kept a large number of horses for hire.

right
John Palmer's
Bath mail coach
in 1784

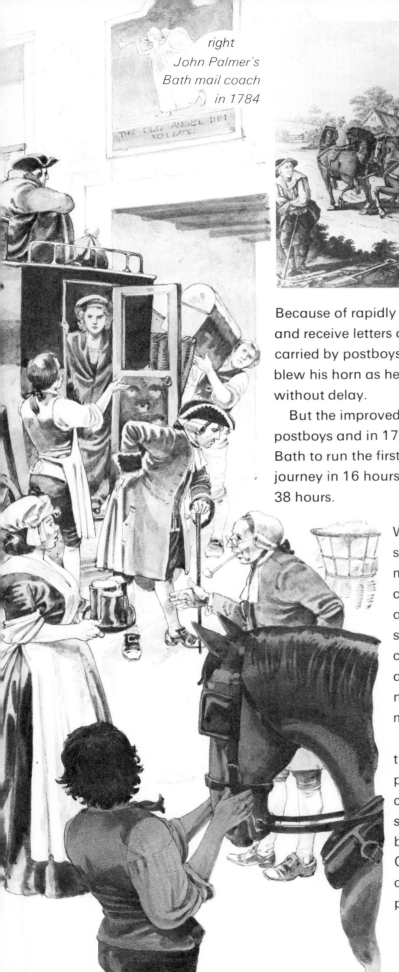

Because of rapidly increasing trade, business men needed to send and receive letters quickly. For hundreds of years letters had been carried by postboys on horseback. The postboy paid no tolls, so blew his horn as he approached the tollgate and was let through without delay.

But the improved coaches could travel much faster than the postboys and in 1784 the Post Office allowed John Palmer of Bath to run the first mail coach from London to Bristol. It did the journey in 16 hours, whereas previously the postboys had taken 38 hours.

Within a few years, the fast mail coaches were speeding along the roads between London and most of the main towns. In addition to the coachman and a few passengers, each coach also carried a guard who was armed with a shotgun. It was his duty to protect the mail if the coach was attacked by highwaymen. If an accident occurred, he finished the journey to the next stage on one of the horses, or on foot, to make sure the mail was delivered safely.

The mail coaches kept to a strict timetable and their coachmen took a great pride in arriving punctually at each stage. Their horses were changed about every 11 kilometres to keep up the speed and there was only time for a quick snack before the mail coach was on its way again. On a long journey the coachman, too, was often changed and he expected a tip from his passengers before he left them.

Canals

As trade increased during the 18th century, men began to move more goods about the country than ever before. But many roads were still bad and transport by packhorses and wagons was slow and expensive. Some heavy goods, such as coal and iron, were sent round the coasts by sea. Others were carried along the rivers, but over the years many of these had filled up with mud and become too shallow.

In 1759 the Duke of Bridgewater asked an engineer called James Brindley to build a canal to carry coal from his coalmine at Worsley to Manchester, about seven miles away. It was later extended to Runcorn, on the River Mersey, so that coal could be taken to the large ships at the port of Liverpool.

People began to realise that canals would enable goods to be sent from one place to another more cheaply than by road. Brindley next built the Grand Trunk Canal which joined up industrial towns in the Midlands to the rivers Trent and Mersey. Other canals followed and soon a network of canals linked together rivers over most of the country.

James Brindley had little education, but was a very clever engineer.

Here is a picture of the Rolle Canal in Devon. Notice:
—the canal boats being towed along by horses
—the men leading the horses along the towpath beside the canal
—the high bridge carrying the canal over the river below. This special type of bridge is called an aqueduct. James Brindley used an aqueduct to carry the Bridgewater Canal over the River Irwell.
—the men on the boats. It took two men to 'leg' the boat through a tunnel. The men laid on boards across the boat and pushed against the wall of the tunnel with their legs.

The coming of the railways

Since about the year 1600 coal wagons had been pulled along wooden rails by horses and from the middle of the 18th century iron rails were being used. These early 'rail-ways' moved coal from the mines to the rivers and canals, where it was loaded into barges.

In 1803 the first public railway was opened. This was the Surrey Iron Railway and ran between Croydon and Wandsworth. Anyone could carry goods along it in his own wagon if he paid tolls to the owners.

Until then, the steam engines in factories were too large and clumsy to be used on railways, but in 1804 Richard Trevithick built the first steam locomotive to run on rails at an ironworks in South Wales.

In 1808 Trevithick demonstrated this engine on a circular track near Euston Square in London. It was called 'Catch-me-who-can'.

After this, other engineers began to build steam locomotives for the colliery railways in the north of England. They went very slowly (not much faster than you could walk) and they often broke down.

Here is a picture of the opening of the Stockton and Darlington Railway on 27th September 1825. This was the first public steam railway to carry passengers as well as goods between two towns. At first horse-drawn coaches could also use the railway track, but later it became too busy for horse traffic.

George Stephenson, the colliery engineer who had built the Stockton and Darlington railway, was next asked to build a railway between Liverpool and Manchester. Tolls on the Bridgewater Canal had been raised and local businessmen now thought it was too slow and expensive.

Stephenson had a more difficult task this time, for part of the railway line had to be laid over a muddy bog at Chat Moss. However, he solved the problem by laying hurdles and brushwood on the bog and covering them with stones and gravel. The railway took over three years to complete.

Before the railway opened, the owners held a trial at Rainhill to discover the best engine. Four locomotives took part, but only the *Rocket*, which was built and driven by George Stephenson, finished the course and won the prize of £500. Because of this only Stephenson's engines, including the *Rocket*, were used on the new railway.

Stephenson's 'Rocket' which can be seen at the Science Museum in London

Here is the opening of the Liverpool and Manchester railway on 15th September 1830.
Notice:
—the passenger coaches on the left of the picture
—Stephenson's engines with their tall chimneys and barrel-shaped boilers
—the well-dressed guests in the centre of the picture. Later, one of them fell on the line and was run over by the *Rocket* and killed.

The new railway carried both passengers and goods and was a great success. Within a few years many others were built as people began to realise that railway travel was much faster than anything before.

Things to do

1 Draw pictures and write notes in your book about:
   a) the coming of machines
   b) inside the factories
   c) down the mines
   d) canals
   e) early railways.

2 Paint large wall pictures of:
   a) a factory town
   b) a stage coach arriving at an inn
   c) the Stockton and Darlington Railway.

3 Make models of:
   a) *HMS. Victory*
   b) a tollgate and tollhouse
   c) Stephenson's *Rocket*.

4 Imagine you travelled on a mail coach between London and Bristol and write an account of your journey. Describe the coachman, the guard and your fellow passengers. Say what happened at the inns when the horses and sometimes the coachman were changed, how you were stopped by a highwayman, but how the mail eventually reached Bristol.

5 Use books in your library to find out more about:
   a) James Watt
   b) James Brindley
   c) Thomas Telford
   d) George Stephenson.

Collect together all your notes, pieces of writing, models, charts, maps, pictures and friezes. Make an exhibition of your work with the title Tudor, Stuart and Georgian Times. Invite children from other classes to see your exhibition and tell them about your work.

Now that you have come to the end of this book try to find out more about the people who lived in those days. There are several *Focus on History* books which will help you and you may find others in your local library.

Many museums, and houses which are open to the public, contain things from Tudor, Stuart and Georgian times. These help us to learn more about the way people lived, worked and played. Visit as many of these buildings as you can and make drawings and notes about what you find there. Collect guide-books, postcards and colour slides and make yourself an expert on life in England at that time.

In 1837 William IV died and his niece Victoria became Queen. She was only 18 years old and her reign was to last for the next 64 years.

Index